One for the Pot

FRED TAYLOR'S
GAME AND FISH
COOKBOOK

Ashford, Buchan & Enright
Leatherhead, Surrey

First Published 1979
A and C Black (Publishers) Ltd
35 Bedford Row London WC1R 4JH

First Paperback Edition 1992
Published by Ashford, Buchan & Enright
31 Bridge Street, Leatherhead, Surrey

ISBN 1 85253 266 1

Taylor, Frederick James
One for the pot.
1. Cookery (Fish)
2. Cookery (Game)
I. Title
641.6'9 TX747

ISBN 1 85253 266 1

Typeset by Priory Publications, Haywards Heath
Printed in Great Britain by FotoDirect Ltd, Brighton

CONTENTS

Dedication

To the memory of my brother Ken
who shared the outdoors
and its many bounties with me
for almost half a century."

Preface
to the Second Edition

The first edition of this little book was incomplete. So, too, is this second and expanded edition. It will never be quite complete because there will always be afterthoughts, new ideas and suggestions to consider. I have never stopped learning about 'wild' food nor have I ever stopped thinking up new ideas of preparing it. My original suggestion that cooking is a simple, commonsense procedure still applies. I never intended this to be a recipe book and, although I have included a few more in this edition, they remain as vague and as flexible as the earlier ones. Only where accuracy is essential to produce such items as pies and puddings have I given weights or measures and, even then, there is a fair amount of leeway.

I was once sent a letter from a woman friend of the family thanking me for her copy of *One for the Pot*. She referred to it as a 'recipe book' which at once proved to me that she had not bothered to open it. Our relationship has never been quite the same since!

My old friend, the late Richard Walker, told me often that he was in the habit of referring to *One for the Pot* for ideas on how to cook various products. That really was my reason for writing it. To suggest ideas that may be altered or even improved upon, to suit the time, the place and the basic main ingredients. That is the fun of game and fish cookery. It need never become boring.

I have included in this edition some more thoughts on outdoor cooking, by which I mean true camp fire cooking. I have done so because I believe modern barbecue units have encouraged more people to enjoy cooking in the open air. The skills of campfire cooking have been lost to some extent because of camp sites and caravan parks where 'hook-ups' to gas, water and electricity are available.

Those who pull into such places claim to have 'been camping' but I truly wonder why they bother!

Each to his own, of course. It is not for me, although I confess that I have found such places convenient when travelling in the Antipodes. The gap between barbecue cooking and camp fire cooking is not desperately wide and the hot 'coals' of a burned-down camp fire are very similar to commercial charcoal. They have a number of advantages over briquettes, however, one of which has to do with cost. Campfire wood in the shape of fallen timber is free! There is a great deal of satisfaction to be derived from the primitive approach and the smell of wood smoke in the open air does much to improve the appetite.

May yours remain keen irrespective of how or where you choose to cook your quarry.

FRED. J. TAYLOR

INTRODUCTION

I WAS ALWAYS brought up not to waste food. 'To waste is a sin,' my mother would say, and in later years my training in bakery, confectionery and general catering bore out what she said. I learned then that waste was not only sinful but unprofitable too. That is possibly why I become very angry with people who shoot game (in the loosest sense of the word) that they have no intention of eating or of giving away to be eaten. I become just as angry with people who catch fish and leave them to rot on the bank. It happens every year. A pigeon is chucked in the ditch 'because one's not worth taking back'; a hare is left in the ploughing because 'they're too strong' or 'too bloody' , or 'too heavy to lug around'. A pike is tossed into the bushes because 'they're too bony'; a catch of grayling is left in a heap on the riverside because 'they're too muddy' or 'too much trouble to clean'.

I only hear these stories second hand, of course; I do not allow such things to happen when I'm around myself. It so happens that one wood pigeon can be transformed into a magnificent meal for two people. A hare does not have to be too strong or too bloody and while I do not deny that it is heavy to lug around I've never yet failed to struggle back with one. Pike are bony but there are ways of dressing them so that most of the bones are left with the skin and carcase. I have yet to encounter a muddy-tasting grayling and in view of the fact that all of mine are caught exclusively from chalk streams, I doubt if I ever shall. The edibility of fish and game depends so much on preparation and cooking that it is small wonder I hear bad reports from dissatisfied people.

'I don't like fresh water fish,' they say, and order stew-fed rainbow trout when they eat out. I can only conclude that they have no taste buds or that they have no culinary imagination. I use the word imagination advisedly because the home cooking of fish and game requires just that and little else.

When I was churning out chocolate gateaux, rock cakes and cream buns as a professional I had to work to a formula. The housewife calls it a recipe, but it's the same thing by a different name. A formula takes into account *exact weights, consistent* results, costings down to a fraction of a penny, and profit margins. A recipe as used by the housewife, if followed exactly, produces the same result on each and every occasion. Fair enough. There's nothing wrong with that provided there are enough *different* recipes to prevent boredom. When one cook says to another 'This is delicious, please let me have your recipe,' she is paying a great compliment. It is only fitting that the recipe should change hands because it is an essential part of fish and game cookery, and also the reason for many developing friendships. But not all country cooking is subject to recipes or formulae. A degree of artistry and experiment can make the whole deal a lot more exciting. Sadly, most cooks are scared to be adventurous, and after a time even their most superbly presented dishes pale a little. Basic knowledge of cookery is obviously essential in the preparation of all meals but, just as the professional musician can switch from 'automatic pilot' to artistic improvisation, so should the cook be able to express his or her artistic ability.

Let's look at fish first. In so many circumstances fresh water fish such as brown and rainbow trout are ruined before they reach the kitchen. They are left to dry out in the sun, become fly blown or broil in plastic bags and car boots. They are left with the guts in overnight and only attended to when they are on the verge of being ruined. Small wonder some people say they 'don't like trout - they taste muddy'. Sacrilege I call it, *and* sinful waste. Cleaned, gilled and washed in the stream, kept on a stringer in cold running water, or put into a portable cooler box containing ice, the flavour of those same fish would have been out of this world. That part of the preparation should be done by the fisherman, at the water's edge, and not by the cook at home later. The best cook in the world cannot make a bad fish good.

All fish can be filleted as long as they're big enough, and by that I mean weighing upwards of half a pound. It takes a number of half pound grayling to make a meal, but why not? Most grayling are located in numbers, most are looked upon as undesirables and there's no earthly reason why a dozen or more fish should not be filleted before cooking. They are winter fish, of course, and at that time of year it is not so essential to dress out fish quite as quickly.

A *sharp* knife is essential, and it should have a flexible blade to follow the rib cage closely. Filleting fish looks wasteful but in fact it is not. Very little edible flesh is left if the job is done properly.

I'd hate to have traditional trout dishes served up week after week (we eat trout once a week the whole year round) and for that very reason I've always been willing to experiment. In the process I've stumbled across ways of cooking them that can be applied to pike, grayling, perch and, if you're fortunate enough to catch them, sea-trout, salmon, and almost any sea fish.

Most cooks I know are either scared or horrified at the thought of filleting a salmon - but why not? Salmon fillets are easy to freeze, take up less freezer room and do not encourage waste. The head and remainders can be cooked up for basic sauces and a fish that's really too big for a small family can then be fixed a dozen different ways. It takes a little practice to become efficient at filleting, but it really is worth the effort. The diagrams in the Pike chapter, redrawn from photographs I took to illustrate Fred Buller's fine book *Pike* (wherein are contained some fine pike recipes), show the simplest way of doing it. Strictly speaking the bones of the rib cage should not be cut through as shown, but followed round with a flexible fillet knife. Those minor bones can easily be removed from the fillet later, however, and the same method may be used to deal with such smaller fish as perch, trout and grayling.

Cooking the fish will come later. For the moment I am only concerned with *keeping them fit to cook.*

It's possible that my own thoughts on cooking are different from those of many experienced shots, gourmets, gamekeepers or culinary artists, but they may suit others who are willing to break from tradition. I've been called an inverted snob because I do not care to hang pheasants from January to Easter, and because I do not enjoy high game or food cooked in wine. If that makes me an inverted snob then I am one; but I cannot change my views. I include ways and means of preparing such food in this book. I am well capable of such cooking, but I do not have to like it.

I do not believe it is sacrilegious to prepare dishes containing a mixture of game. My game pies are never the same because they are the result of accumulations rather than recipes. But they taste pretty good and I have recommendations to prove it! Traditional English 'game' dishes are undoubtedly excellent, and in this age of the deep-freeze can be eaten as and when fancy dictates. Today, the shooting man can stock up with game for the whole year, and while this is good when looked upon with economics in mind, it does tend to take away some of the old anticipations we once experienced. The gardener does the same with his fresh vegetables, and as a result the early summer's first picking of broad beans, young carrots and garden peas is not quite as mouth-watering as it used to be. So, with game available at any time, different ideas of cooking it have to be considered. But where to start?

Pies made up of what in the game book might be called 'various' provide a means of using up excess game and making more room in the freezer. They can be produced as 'cold cut' pies with hard boiled eggs and jelly, or as hot, main-meal dishes. Several can be made and deep frozen for quick meals later in the year. There's no end to what can be done.

Looking back over the years I can recall many experiments regarding game cookery and there's no doubt that I have applied my own mother's down-to-earth methods to them.

When we were kids we ate moorhen, pigeon and rabbit in the same pie or casserole, usually because there was one of each and not enough to go round individually. Today I put all kinds of game into a brawn for cold cuts and relish the different flavours offered.

One of my favourites, for example, is rabbit brawn. Half rabbit, half lean bacon, thyme and seasoning, with a trotter or a teaspoonful of gelatine to make it all set in the mould. Nothing fancy, nothing difficult, and it's not likely to go wrong because of incorrect weighing. If it doesn't set just boil it up again and add a bit more gelatine. This is the kind of cooking I am interested in and it forms the basis of this book. There are recipes, it's true, but they are vague and flexible. The dishes involved will not be ruined if the recipes are not adhered to and they will possibly be improved by a little imagination on the reader's part. I am only concerned with proving that you do not have to be an Escoffier or Mrs Beaton to turn out an excellent meal, and to convince you that there is very little inedible 'game'. I have never eaten hedgehog, though I know people who have and still do today. I once had an uncle who would shoot and eat herons, though his stock remark was that 'there's no more meat on 'em than a thrush'.

Years ago I shot, and turned into pies, literally hundreds, perhaps thousands, of starlings. Starling shoots were commonplace when I was a boy and the practice continued for a year or two after the war when food was short. We hoped for, and usually achieved, a bag of between twelve and twenty which, with some shin beef and occasionally some beef kidney, helped make a large meal for a large family. I remember once having six starlings and six snipe in the same pudding (only the breasts and legs were used) and hardly knowing which was which in the eating.

Good old days? Bad old days? It's a job to say. By today's standards perhaps they were bad, but at least they were days of full and plenty when others less fortunate were hungry. They taught us how to survive lean times, and I believe they made us all better sportsmen in later years. I'm glad to have experienced them.

If nothing else they taught me to appreciate game and fish dishes and I quickly learned that a little care in the field helped make the meat more palatable in the cooked dish.

Rabbits, for example, are better if hung up in the field until they cool off and stiffen. By keeping them separate and not bunching them, by hanging them in shade and out of a wintry sun, the process is hastened. *Then*, when the carcases are cold, they can be field dressed by removing the intestines and stomach. The lungs and other remainders can be removed when they are skinned later. It is wise to 'thumb' rabbits towards the vent before dressing out. The slight pressure imposed forces out the urine and prevents the bladder from being punctured with the gutting knife. If this happens the meat can become unpleasantly tainted if not washed off at once (see diagram).

These are the small things that make so much difference to the finished dish but they really are only common sense.

The same kind of thinking can be applied to all kinds of game and fish. It is not necessary always to field dress, of course. Pheasant, hare, partridge, and other game (in the truest sense of the word) are better if not so treated, but they should be hung in a cool place, and kept out of game bags as much as possible.

Game and fish, if looked after in the early stages, will undoubtedly reach the table all the better for the effort.

The following *'Terms of Carving both Fish, Fowl and Flesh'* appeared in *The Accomplished Lady's Delight*, first published in 1675.

Barb a lobster
Chine a Salmon
Culpon a trout
Sauce a capon or tench
Splay that bream
Splat that pike
Thigh a pigeon
Unbrace a mallard
Unlace a coney
Sauce a plaice or flounder
String that lamprey
Transon that eel

These extracts were taken from the second edition which appeared in 1677. The work is attributed to Mrs Hannah Wooley, who compiled it from the works of Thomas Barker, Izaak Walton and John Denny.

SAUCES AND GRAVIES

ALL MEAT, fish or game can be suitably altered, dressed-up or improved by an appropriate sauce. Poor products can never be made perfect, stale products can never be made fresh, but there are ways and means of using sauces to make interesting differences to any dish. Besides which, tough meat and game can be made tender if stewed or casseroled in a tasty sauce. In many cases a simple gravy addition to a roast bird or rabbit is enough. A hint of the buttery liquid that has seeped out from a cooking trout or salmon will moisten it and improve its taste. On many occasions it would be unwise to add more than a little lemon juice to it. If game such as hare is casseroled or jugged in the manner described later in the book, the sauce is produced naturally and as both meat and sauce mature together as a result of the cooking and continue to do so for as long as it cooks, there is, perhaps, no better way of achieving a fine end product.

There are, however, a large number of sauces, thick and thin, brown and white, which can be used either as 'pour-overs' or 'cook-ins'. Most can be used for both. These are based on a roux made from equal weights of plain flour and fat in the form of butter, margarine, dripping, lard or oil.

Without being too fussy about it, white sauces need a white roux made from margarine and/or butter, and brown sauces need a brown roux made from lard, dripping, white fat or stock skimmings. That's a generalisation, and as such could be faulted by an expert trying to prove a point. But it will stand up to any test and will never spoil a dish.

The principles are simple, but, unlike most other dishes in this book, they call for fairly accurate measurements at the outset. In other words, we have to resort to recipes.

BASIC WHITE SAUCE

Melt 1 oz of butter or margarine and stir in 1 oz of plain white flour. If, like me, you prefer to use wholemeal flour for all kinds of cooking, do not be afraid to use it for a white sauce. The final product will not be strictly white but it will be a better-tasting sauce.

Cook together slowly, without allowing the flour to brown, and when thoroughly mingled remove from the heat. This white roux now has to be added to the stock being used. It could be milk, fish stock, clear bone stock or vegetable stock. One pint of stock will usually absorb a 2 oz roux, but obviously some differences in consistency will be called for from time to time and the amount of stock added can be increased or reduced to make a thinner or thicker sauce. If additions such as full cream are considered necessary to enrich a basic sauce, this will have to be allowed for and adjustment made to the stock quantity.

BASIC BROWN SAUCE

A brown sauce is made in exactly the same way except that the roux is allowed to cook longer and over a higher heat. It is stirred continually until it takes on a brown colour. How brown depends upon you, the cook. If it is left to turn to a dark chocolate colour, a rich brown sauce will result. Generally speaking brown sauces are used for dark meats, but there is no reason for not using them with pheasant, rabbit, and other light-coloured meats. Good meat or bone stock, with or without diced vegetables, should then be added. A darker sauce will result if the raw bones used for stock (and these include the bones from hare, pheasant, rabbit, pigeon and other game) are browned off in the oven beforehand.

Some cooks experience difficulty in adding the roux to the stock (or vice versa) and complain of lumpy sauces. The answer is simple. Do not add boiling stock to a cooking roux. Add boiling stock to a cold roux, or cold stock to a cooking roux. Do it slowly, add the stock a little at a time and keep stirring.

And what if it does go lumpy? Grab the egg whisk, poke it into the sauce and churn away. The lumps will surrender unconditionally.

I have not mentioned seasonings for these basic sauces. Obviously salt and pepper will be needed but seasoning is a personal thing and as these sauces form only the basis for literally hundreds of others, it is impossible to go too deeply into the subject.

So, having described simple white and brown sauces, and having accepted that, generally speaking, white sauces go with fish and white meat, while brown sauces go with darker meats, I'll have done with basic recipes for the time being. Later I will outline a few practical recipes for 'cook-in' sauces, but in the meantime think of what you might add to a basic sauce to make your fish or meat more attractive.

And bear in mind that, in the main, it is only necessary to lay your fish, game, wildfowl or venison into a casserole dish, cover with a favourite sauce and let it take care of itself.

A few chopped prawns, chopped eggs, grated cheese, a little salad dressing, a hint of anchovy essence, a touch of tomato purée or a squeeze of lemon juice are *just a few* of the simple, everyday things which may be added to an ordinary white sauce before cooking fish of any kind. You may use them singly or you may put in several additions to suit your mood or taste.

Curry powder, paprika, red wine, garlic, red peppers, tomato juice, wine vinegar, brown sugar, sliced mushrooms, tabasco or tomato ketchup may all be used to liven up a dull brown sauce. I've only touched on a few simple additions; you may dream up a hundred more. Be cautious, of course, but do not be afraid to experiment. Game and fish dishes offer incredible scope for just that. And remember, too, that there are readily available 'cook-in' sauces in the shape of ordinary tinned soups. The busy housewife who needs time for other jobs will find that rabbit, hare, wild duck, partridge, pheasant, any game in fact, will cook nicely in the oven if covered with diluted tinned soup. Some chopped onions and/or carrots may be included if desired but they are not strictly necessary.

I would not presume to tell you what soup to use with which kind of game because tastes vary. I will say that I have enjoyed rabbit cooked in tomato soup, mushroom soup and chicken soup. I have had pigeon and hare cooked in oxtail soup and I have thoroughly enjoyed pheasant breasts cooked in asparagus soup. But don't take my word for it. Try some of them yourself and don't be afraid to slice a few potatoes over the top, or grate some cheese, or add a little spaghetti or put in a dumpling, or cover with a pie crust. Who cares if it's 'in the book' or 'the done thing'? What matters is that it's easy, tasty and convenient to cook game this way. It is wide open to all kinds of 'artistry', and almost impossible to spoil!

SOME SPECIFIC SAUCE RECIPES

Shrimp Sauce (for trout, salmon, etc. as a garnish)

Half a pint of white sauce, 1 oz full cream, 1 dessertspoonful of lemon juice, 1 oz butter, I lb finely chopped shelled (frozen) shrimps and a little tomato purée (to colour). Make the white sauce hot, stir in the remaining ingredients slowly, keep hot but do not boil. Season with salt and cayenne pepper.

Cucumber Sauce (for any fish as a garnish)

Half a pint of white sauce, about half a regular cucumber, 1 oz butter, 1 small onion or shallot.

Slice the cucumber and onion and cook slowly in the butter, keeping the pan covered. When tender, pass through a sieve (to retain seeds) and add the purée to the white sauce. Season with salt and black pepper. A little lemon juice may be added if desired, and the sauce may be enriched with cream.

Mustard Sauce (originally for herrings, etc, but may be used as a garnish for any fish)

Half a pint of white sauce, 1 level dessertspoonful of mustard powder, one tablespoonful of lemon juice, 1 oz full cream. Make the white sauce hot, mix the mustard powder and lemon juice to a smooth paste, add the cream and stir into the hot sauce. Do not boil. Season with salt and black pepper. Vinegar may be used instead of lemon juice and an interesting variation may be achieved by adding a measure of mixed French mustard to suit your own taste.

Brown Butter (for a white fish garnish)

$\frac{1}{4}$ lb butter, about 1 eggcupful of finely chopped parsley, 1 sherry glassful of dark vinegar, pepper and salt.

Cook the butter until it begins to turn brown and then add the parsley, vinegar, pepper and salt. Continue cooking for another minute before pouring over prepared fish. I only once ate carp in England (though I have eaten it many times in the USA) and on that occasion it was served with brown butter by an expert German cook.

I have used her recipe many times since with other white fish including grayling.

Sardine Sauce (for cooking and adding flavour to any non-game fish)

1 oz butter, 1 small tin of sardines, 1 small onion, 1 bay leaf, a small pinch of nutmeg, 1 tablespoonful of lemon juice, $\frac{3}{4}$ pint of

white sauce (made with fish stock if possible), salt and cayenne pepper.

Slice the onion thinly and cook with the bay leaf in the butter until tender. Add the nutmeg, lemon juice, and seasoning. Remove the bay leaf, add the sardines and warm through. Pass through a blender or sieve and add to the hot white sauce. Pour over any white fish fillets and cook in a moderate oven until the fish is tender.

Curry Sauce (for cooking game or wild fowl)

1 pint of brown sauce, 1 large onion, 1 large carrot, 1 oz butter, 1 tablespoonful curry powder, 1 apple, 2 oz raisins or sultanas, 1 tablespoonful chutney, salt, mustard and black pepper.

Chop the onion and carrot into small dice and cook off in the melted butter. Dust with the curry powder and continue cooking, add the diced apple, raisins, chutney and seasoning and mix all together in the brown sauce.

Cover any game or wild fowl with this sauce and cook slowly in a casserole dish until tender.

Barbecue Sauce (for use as a cook-in sauce for any game or wild fowl)

1 large onion, $\frac{1}{4}$ lb finely minced beef, 1 oz lard or dripping, 1 tablespoonful each of chopped parsley, lemon juice, brown sugar, mixed mustard (English), plain flour, tomato purée, $\frac{1}{2}$ cup tomato ketchup, $\frac{1}{2}$ cup vinegar, salt, paprika and a very little cayenne pepper.

Cook together the minced beef, chopped onion and fat for about 5 minutes. Dust with flour, and then add remaining ingredients. Dilute if necessary with a little stock or water, pour over any game or wild fowl and either casserole or pressure cook until tender. This is a spicy sauce and some adjustments to quantities may be deemed necessary to suit individual tastes.

Parsley Sauce (for all kinds of fish and light meats such as rabbit and pheasant)

1 pint of white sauce (made from stock and milk), salt, red pepper and two tablespoonfuls of chopped fresh parsley.

Bring the sauce to the boil, season and remove from heat. Stir· in the chopped parsley and do not re-boil.

If used as a 'cook-in' sauce for rabbit, trout, pike, etc., leave out the parsley and add it just before serving.

Orange Sauce (for wild duck as a garnish)

2 oranges, 1 pint of thick white sauce, the juice of a lemon, 1 small glass of red wine or port, salt and pepper.

Bring the white sauce to the boil, add the juice from the oranges and the lemon. Grate the rind of one orange into the sauce and allow all to cook slowly and reduce. Just before serving add the wine and season to taste. There are many variations to this recipe and it may be improved by the addition of redcurrant jelly and/or the juices from the freshly roasted bird.

Sage and Onion Sauce (for rabbit, pheasant or any true game bird)

1 large onion, ½ pint brown sauce, ½ oz pork dripping or lard, 2 oz fine bread crumbs, 1 teaspoonful dried sage, salt and black pepper.

Chop the onions and cook until brown in the lard, stir in the sage and breadcrumbs and add all to the hot brown sauce. Season to taste. This sauce serves also as an excellent cook-in sauce if diluted with stock.

There are, of course, hundreds more. Some are complicated (in my opinion unnecessarily so), some very simple. Some only serve as garnish or 'gravy' type sauces; others can be used as a basis for cooking in casserole, stew jar or pressure cooker. I have put my suggestions above down in recipe form for convenience and to give some idea of quantities required but there is no need to adhere strictly to the quantities recommended. Variety, they say, is the spice of life.

PASTES, DOUGHS AND FORCEMEATS

YOU CAN MAKE almost anything into a pie by putting a pastry crust over it, and you might say the same about puddings.

There are several different types of pastry, but there is really only one basic kind of pudding dough. You can make a pudding or dumpling dough richer by adding more fat, or by cracking eggs into the mix, but most simple, savoury pudding mixes taste better if they are not too rich. If you put too much fat into a pudding dough, it becomes pastry and a pastry mix doesn't make a good pudding crust or dumpling.

Pastry, for the purposes of this book, can be contained under three headings: (1) short crust; (2) flaky; and (3) hot water.

Let's not get too technical and say that there's a difference between flaky pastry and puff pastry, or between French pastry and shortbread, and choux paste and all the many other kinds known by the expert cook. We're not trying to become expert pastry cooks;

we're figuring out some simple ways of making fish and game more tasty.

Some of the ways of using the various pastes, doughs and forcemeats are discussed in the following chapters, but for the time being let's look into how they're made.

(1) SHORT CRUST PASTRY

1 lb plain flour, ½ lb lard or beef dripping, salt, water to mix.

Rub the fat into the flour and salt until it is of the so-called 'oatmeal consistency'. Then add water, mixing lightly and with an upwards motion until a workable paste is formed. I won't give water quantities because flours differ a great deal.

This is plain, good, old-fashioned, short, pie-crust pastry. You can take out a little of the fat and add a pinch of baking powder if you want to make it slightly less rich. If you want it to brown quickly you may use milk instead of water to mix. You may also use eggs in place of some of the liquid to make a richer paste.

Bear in mind, however, that milk and eggs brown off quickly and that this kind of paste will not do for raw meat pies which have to be baked for an hour or longer at a lower temperature, *after* the initial browning.

All raw meat pie pastry should be mixed with plain water. Beaten egg and/or milk will serve to provide a brown glaze later. There is little point in using more than 50 per cent fat in any short crust pastry, but it is worth recording that reasonable pastry can be made using considerably less. The higher the fat content (up to 50 per cent) the more 'kneading' the pastry will tolerate, but it should always be handled as little as possible.

(2) FLAKY PASTRY

Making puff or flaky pastry without the proper margarine used by professional bakers is, in my opinion, more trouble than it's worth. Puff pastry can be bought ready-made from most bakers and some supermarkets and I do not believe it is possible to produce a technically better paste at home.

But it is possible to make better tasting (though infinitely more time-consuming) pastry if you're prepared to suffer for it. You need 1 lb flour (plain), 1 lb hard butter or margarine (despite what many so-called experts would have you believe, margarine is more plastic and less inclined to go oily than butter and as such makes better pastries and cakes. The only possible advantage of using butter lies in the reputed 'quality' or 'taste').

I'm not going to go into the umpteen different ways of making puff paste here. I'll tell you one simple way and leave the rest to you.

Mix the salt and flour together in a big bowl. Cut up the hard margarine into 1 in. cubes and stir them into the flour. Have the flour cold to start with and work in a cool place. Use iced water in preference to tepid. The object is to mix the flour into a dough without rubbing in or dissolving the margarine.

When you have a knobby, sticky, margarine-studded dough, tip it out on to a floured board (or a marble slab is better if you have one). Roll it out into a long sheet (a bottle of iced water is the best possible rolling pin). It's hard work and you need not be afraid to 'sock it to it' a time or two!

When you have a long, narrow strip, fold both ends to the middle and then fold it in half again. Turn the block 90o to the right and roll out another long strip. Fold again as before and then put the block in the refrigerator for at least half an hour. Repeat the process three more times with rests in between and you should have a good quality flaky pastry.

Roll it out to cover whatever it's supposed to cover, and then *leave it in the warm kitchen for about 20 minutes before baking.* That way you'll have no shrinkage or distortion.

You may be able to buy puff pastry margarine from your baker. If you can, do so. It will make better paste, it needs only a short rest period between folds, and it does not have to be kept cold. It does, however, end up as a better flaky or puff pastry if it is given the twenty-minute rest period before baking.

It too can be glazed with egg and/or milk, and it should be baked off in a hot (450°F) oven to get the initial lift.

(3) HOT WATER PASTRY

To $\frac{1}{4}$ pint boiling salted water add 6 oz lard and cook until it has dissolved completely. While still boiling, add 1 lb of plain flour and stir over the heat until a smooth workable paste is formed and the sides of the saucepan are clear. This paste is not often used in game cooking, but it makes an excellent casing and crust for what are commonly called hand-raised pies. They are really very simple to produce but the game meat filling usually requires the addition of a little extra fat.

(4) PUDDING DOUGH

1 lb self-raising flour (or plain flour with the appropriate amount of baking powder, which is about 1 heaped teaspoonful), $\frac{1}{4}$ lb suet, salt, and water to mix to a workable dough. That's it! You simply stir in the salt and suet, pour in the water and mix lightly. Don't pound the daylights out of pudding dough, it can't take it. Add a little more suet if you like a rich crust that clings to the roof of your mouth, otherwise stick with the 4-1 ratio of flour and suet. By all means substitute lard, white fat, dripping or margarine for the suet if it is more convenient. You will have to rub it in pastry fashion before adding the water, of course.

This basic mix will serve for dumplings or puddings, and although it is mainly a product for slow cooking and steaming, there are recipes that call for browning off in the oven - as we shall see later in the book.

(5) DAMPER OR SODA BREAD

Having written extensively about wilderness and outback cooking here and there, I now learn that many anglers and outdoor sportsmen are interested in 'baking the damper' as practised in the Australian bush country. In the early pioneering days, the damper was baked in the hot ashes of a camp fire. It was seen to rise and form a crust beneath its covering of ash and, when removed, was tapped all over with a stick to free it from its hot dust. Having been liberally dusted with flour and insulated to some extent from the ashes by another sprinkling of flour, a damper will remain reasonably free from ash or charcoal if tended correctly. It is better baked in a Dutch camp oven (of which more later) but it can be baked in an ordinary oven. It is, in fact, simply a traditional soda bread loaf as still made by many housewives today. It is a fitting accompaniment to any kind of game or fish and is just about 1000 per cent more tasty than some of the ghastly and utterly inedible concoctions I have eaten in the guise of so-called sliced bread. That, of course, is a personal opinion!

The damper, in its simplest of forms, comprises a dough made from plain flour, baking powder, salt and water. Directions as to how much to use are certain to be found on each packet of baking powder. Plain flour becomes self-raising flour with the addition of baking powder and the most convenient procedure today would be to use self-raising flour at the outset. If I use it, however, I cheat a little and add an extra pinch of baking powder. It lifts the damper just that little bit more and makes for a lighter loaf. Beware of adding too much, however. That will result in a lighter loaf that carries a noticeable taint.

Salt, at the rate of about 1 teaspoon to 1lb. of flour, may be added either to the water or the flour before mixing the dough. Weights and measures are not otherwise necessary because liquid and dry ingredients are blended to make a mouldable dough. I use half milk and half water if possible, simply because it browns the crust off more quickly. Damper can be varied by the addition of an ounce of lard and/or a little sugar to make the end product a little more scone-like, but I prefer to use just the basic ingredients.

Wherever the damper is baked, it will benefit from having a wet top. Moistened thoroughly with water and patted down, the dough will tend to rise that little bit extra before the crust has had time to form. Cutting a fairly deep cross in a round, moulded damper, will improve the crust of the end product.

The same dough may be made into flat 'rolls' and cooked on a plate barbecue or in a heavy iron skillet. They need turning frequently and are not strictly bread rolls as such when cooked, but they are superb if eaten when still warm.

(6) SOURDOUGH

The damper, as just described, offers a quickly-made and convenient alternative to shop-bought bread but it is not to be compared with the crisp and nutty-flavoured bread which may be made by using yeast.

There are a million recipes for making bread. They are to be found in magazines and cook books, and on the backs of flour bags or yeast packs. Yeast comes in many forms and it is possible to make your own if you wish, but nothing, in my opinion, beats the regular compressed yeast as used by master bakers. It is not always convenient to use or keep for long periods and there is a case for using the dried or desiccated products readily available today. My only comment is: Read the instructions. Some of these yeasts are not meant to be used traditionally.

What is, perhaps, not so widely appreciated is the fact that where yeast is to be used regularly over a period, it is only necessary to have enough on hand for, say, two bread batches. I am referring here to the sourdough principle which involves the topping up of half the yeast used today and leaving it to double its size by tomorrow. In theory and with a constant, regular application, one ounce of yeast will last for ever. My interest in the principle has nothing to do with economy but with the flavour of the finished product and the convenience of all that is involved.

It is not as complicated as I have possibly made it appear. What is needed is a starter. The starter is made up of two cups of flour, two cups of lukewarm water and, say, one ounce of yeast. The quantity of yeast doesn't matter except that too much will work too quickly and too little will take too long. Bear with me!

Put all three ingredients into a plastic lemonade bottle after mixing them thoroughly. Shake the bottle vigorously to mix all well and loosen the cap. Place it in a draught-free spot at room temperature (or a little warmer such as in an airing cupboard) and leave overnight. It is advisable to set the bottle in a bowl or dish because a half-bottle of starter will almost certainly overflow. I prefer to use a big bottle and to keep it no more than one quarter full.

In the morning, take half of the starter, which should now be frothy and yeasty, to make the bread. Simply add salt and enough strong flour to form a workable dough. It is essential to knead it well and to keep it soft rather than tight. You can, if you wish, add more water, salt and flour to make a bigger dough but it will take longer to prove or rise. After it has risen to double its size, knock the dough back to its original size, mould it into loaf shapes and wait for it to rise again. It should be covered with a moist cloth while this is going on and it should again be double its original size before it is baked at around 400°F to 450°F. When it has a crisp crust and sounds hollow when tapped, it is cooked.

In the meantime, replenish the starter bottle with one cup of flour and one cup of water. Shake vigorously to mix all ingredients and, next day, repeat the process using half the starter. In the event that the starter is not needed on a certain day, it can be stored in a refrigerator and used a day or two later. There is a limit to its keeping qualities, however, and eventually the yeast will die. For most general purposes and as a superb accompaniment for all kinds of game, fish and wildfowl dishes, the sourdough loaf remains, in my opinion, unbeatable. My only advice regarding the use of sourdough starters is that you must have time to allow it to develop at its own pace. Attempts to speed up the process can only result in dismal failure but a hot, crusty, sourdough loaf will enhance a simple country meal, game or whatever, to the point of total jubilation.

(7) FORCEMEATS

Most forcemeat or stuffing recipes call for dry breadcrumbs, onions, suet or fat, seasoning and herbs. Those ready-mixed stuffings which may be purchased in packet form are convenient and contain dehydrated materials which reconstitute when moistened. For the busy housewife they are adequate, but they may also be used as tasty additions to home-made forcemeats.

My own ideas of forcemeats are slightly different. I will not conform to recipes and I refuse to become involved in the tiresome business of grating or crumbling stale bread for the basic mix. Nor will I become involved in strict weights or measures because, once again, I emphasise that seasonings, dressings, stuffings, forcemeats (call them what you will) are dishes that do not require rigid quality control.

I will outline here how I make mine, and I will suggest some other additions to the basic ingredients. Then I'll ask you to use your own imagination, which is of much more importance than a set of scales or a measuring cup.

Soak any available stale bread, brown or white, leaving the crust intact, in *cold water* until it is completely saturated. Squeeze it out as dry as possible between your fingers, place it into a big bowl and 'fluff it up'.

Add finely chopped or minced onions, suet, lard or dripping, salt, pepper and any herbs that take your fancy. (Sage alone will give you traditional sage and onion stuffing for example.) Mix all well together and use to enhance game birds, rabbits, venison, fish or wild fowl.

If it feels too sloppy, add a sprinkling of packet stuffing or some really dry breadcrumbs to tighten it.

That's it. A basic, tasty forcemeat with a hundred uses.

And now let's think about one or two variations to take away the boredom and add a little excitement to what is, after all, a typically British dish.

Mixed herbs will give a complete change of flavour. So will thyme and parsley. So will dried chives and celery seed. So will rosemary, so will ... but need I go on? Already the possibilities should be recognisable.

Finely minced beef, pork, ham or bacon pieces added to the mix will alter the flavour yet again, and also improve 'dry' or over-lean game considerably. The hearts, liver and kidneys of rabbit or hare may be minced and added to any basic stuffing. So can the gizzard, heart and liver of game birds or wild fowl.

Onions may be fried before adding them to the bread mix, and finely sliced green leek tops or chopped celery leaves are other useful additions. Minced mushrooms may be added, so may finely chopped peppers. I could fill the book with ideas, but I won't.

If you want a workable forcemeat to use on the *outside* of a game portion (to be discussed later) or to make up into forcemeat balls for frying or serving separately, crack a couple of eggs into the mix and tighten it with more breadcrumbs. Do not be afraid of using extra fat, drippings, or juices from previously cooked joints, fowl or game birds. It adds to the flavour and helps turn a dull old stuffing almost into a meal in its own right.

RABBIT

I THINK I COULD WRITE a whole book about the preparation and cooking of rabbit. I never tire of it. I truly prefer it to pheasant and other game and I'm never short of ideas on how to cook it. There is, however, a time lag between the shooting or catching of the rabbit and its eventual cooking. So much can go wrong during that period that it really is worthwhile taking a few simple precautions both in the field and at home. I have already mentioned briefly that in cold weather rabbits should be gutted in the field *after* they have cooled. They should, as already mentioned, be thumbed to expel the urine from the bladder.

Gutting rabbits that have not cooled is a gory business and when young rabbits are shot during warm weather it is advisable not to do so in the field. It is better to keep them intact and as cool as possible in the circumstances. Precautions against them becoming fly-blown should be taken and it will be found that they will be less likely to attract flies if they are left whole. Gutted rabbits attract flies and with the best will in the world it is difficult to avoid bloodstained hands if they are gutted while still warm.

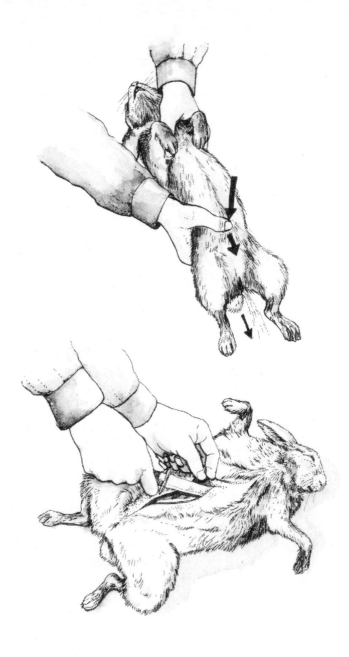

Today, shooting rabbits with a rifle is an accepted practice during the summer months. It is a selective kind of shooting; one that allows a choice between young and old 'game'.

For moral reasons only, the sportsman tries to avoid shooting pregnant does or does in milk. However there is nothing whatever wrong with the meat, and in the event that mistakes are made it need not be wasted.

The usual target for summer shooting, however, is a half to three parts grown youngster and, with an abundance of rabbits available, it is usually possible to pick one off for dinner next day.

Head shots are obviously best because then the edible flesh is not harmed. Taking head shots helps also to avoid wounding and losing rabbits that are apt to kick themselves down the nearest hole.

Nevertheless body shots cannot always be avoided and the of carcase of a rabbit so killed is not the best of sights. But it can be made wholesome as we shall see. First it has to be cleaned and skinned and the removing of the skin is usually indication enough of its tenderness or toughness. If it comes off easily and tears in the process you may be sure your rabbit is tender. If you slip a disc or develop a hernia wrestling with it, you may safely designate it for the stew pot. Rabbits to be kept can be marked before freezing so that mistakes cannot be made in cooking. If you need to make a selection before skinning, however, you can do it by squeezing the jawbones inwards between thumb and forefinger. A tender rabbit will crack at this point; a tough one won't.

A very badly shot rabbit may have to be portioned and the damaged part removed completely, but it is usually sufficient to clean the flesh well under a cold tap and then leave it in *cold* salt water overnight. The congealed blood will dissipate and by morning, after a further washing in clean water, all the meat will be in good shape. Natural pan-dried salt, or block salt if obtainable,

(*Above left*) *'Thumbing out' a rabbit towards the vent.*
(*Left*) *Slitting open the body before gutting.*

is infinitely better than so-called table salt for this purpose. It's better for you too, I'm sure.

So, having skinned and prepared our tender young rabbit, how do we cook it?

Rolled in seasoned flour and cooked in the frying pan along with some crisp bacon or belly pork is one way that really makes up for all the skinning and preparing. It is, I believe, the most delicious game dish of all and I can recall many times when I have risen at 4 am, shot a couple of young rabbits, picked a bag of mushrooms and enjoyed them all for breakfast with my family before 9 am the same morning. Rabbits are perhaps better left for a day before cooking, but if they are cooled (chilled is a better word) quickly and washed thoroughly before cooking they may be eaten within an hour or so.

Out in the Australian bush country I have shot rabbits, dressed them out and spit-roasted them over an open fire for supper immediately.

Roast rabbit is excellent. It should be stuffed with any of the forcemeats mentioned in this book (or your own special favourite) covered with streaky pork and cooked in a hot oven. When the pork has crisped, remove it and allow the rabbit to brown, basting periodically with the natural juices in the roasting dish. Or you can foil cook it in the oven. Lay the rabbit portions on a sheet of foil, smother with chopped onions and bacon or pork, sprinkle with sage, salt and pepper, wrap into a parcel and cook in a hot oven for about an hour. Before serving, open up the foil and allow the contents to crisp.

It is not *wrong* to cook young tender rabbits in pies, stews or casseroles but it always seems to me to be sacrilegious. There will be plenty of adult rabbits later in the year, and many tough old bucks will benefit from slower cooking. Young, tender rabbits should be cooked quickly and, because they are very lean, they should be given the benefit of the fat from some other kind of meat.

Winter rabbits are prime. There is no better sight than that of a dozen cold, stiffened, cleanly dressed rabbits, hanging on a frost-covered blackthorn branch in dead of winter. Nor is there a better tasting meal than a well-cooked fat rabbit. By applying the tests mentioned previously to determine whether or not the rabbit is tough, cook it in any of the following ways.

Lay the portions in a casserole dish, smother with chopped onions and carrots, season and cover with tinned mushroom soup (if it is the concentrated type, dilute first) and cook slowly in the oven. As an alternative, replace the mushroom soup with any of the cook-in sauces already mentioned. If you care to cover the dish with sliced potatoes and/or grated cheese, do so.

To, make a good rabbit pie, stew the rabbit first with onions and carrots. Thicken the stock with a brown roux, place all in a pie dish and cover with short crust pastry. Egg glaze the surface and bake until the pastry is cooked.

Tough rabbit may be cooked in casseroles and stews, or even jugged like hare.

Tender rabbit can be dipped in egg and flour batter and deep fried. It can be dipped into a thin flour and water batter, rolled in breadcrumbs and, again, deep fried.

It can be used, if lightly cooked and pared thinly, as an addition to the bacon in the now very popular Quiche Lorraine. (It was always called egg and bacon pie when we ate it at home.)

Rabbit, in fact, can be cooked in just about any way you care to try, but here are a few slightly different ways of preparing it.

Take the hind legs of a young, tender rabbit, brush over with French mustard and a little pepper and salt. Cut strips of puff pastry about $\frac{3}{4}$ in. wide and spiral them around the legs in 'cream horn' fashion. Brush with egg glaze, cook at 425°F until the pastry rises and browns, then reduce the heat to 350°F until the rabbit is tender.

Alternatively, take the hind legs of several young rabbits and enclose them fully in a covering of forcemeat (sage and onion for instance). Lay them separately in a baking dish, cover with bacon rashers and bake slowly for about $1\frac{1}{2}$ hours. Test with a fork if necessary to see if the rabbit is tender.

Remainders from rabbits deprived of their back legs for these special recipes will serve for stews, pies or puddings. And what could be nicer than an old style rabbit pudding with thick gravy?

Roll the rabbit portions in seasoned flour and place in a lined pudding basin with onions, carrots and mushrooms pressed down tightly. Cover with concentrated stock, seal with a pudding crust lid, cover with a cloth and steam for two hours or just as long as you like after that. You can add stewing beef, kidneys or lean, uncooked ham to change the flavour slightly if you so wish. I have mentioned rabbit brawn in the introductory chapter and, of course, it goes without saying that other game may be mixed with rabbit to ring the changes.

Cold pies are excellent if made from half rabbit and half pork or ham, and here is how I make mine.

Trim the meat from the rabbit and cut into small dice. Pressure-cook the remaining carcase to make a concentrated stock.

Mix the rabbit meat with an equal amount of not-too-lean pork or ham. To each pound of meat add ¼ lb of wholemeal bread (soaked and squeezed). Season liberally with salt, pepper and sage. Pack all into a pie crust made from hot water paste and moulded round an upturned jar. Cover and seal with a lid. Bake for 15 minutes in a 450°F oven, then egg glaze and lower the temperature to 325°F. Cook for another 1½-2 hours, depending upon the size of the pie. Add an ounce of gelatine to a pint of the concentrated stock and pour through the steam vent in the pastry lid. Allow to cool and set before cutting.

Ordinary short crust pastry may be used instead of the hot water pastry if the pie is made in a round cake tin. This is probably an easier procedure for a busy housewife - but it does not look quite as professional as the hand-raised version.

I hope this chapter shows that, without becoming deeply involved in recipes, rabbit need never be boring. I have only discussed a few ways of cooking it here. There are many, many more, and undoubtedly some of the other game dishes described will serve for rabbit also.

Meanwhile here are a few more tried and tested dishes.

Baked whole rabbit (American style)

Soak the rabbit in vinegar and water overnight. Drain off, split open the breast cavity and press flat in a baking dish. Add fried onions, finely chopped mushrooms, a little diced green pepper and about a teaspoonful of brown sugar. Cover with a rich white sauce and bake in a moderate oven until tender.

Rabbit sausage (American style)

Mince finely about 2 lb of raw rabbit meat, and 1 lb raw pork. Add 1 cupful of dry breadcrumbs, an egg, a little sage, salt and paprika. Mix all thoroughly and if too dry moisten with a little milk. Make into sausage or patty shapes and bake in a hot oven or fry in a heavy duty pan.

Barbecue rabbit (American style)

Pressure-cook rabbit portions briefly (tough ones a minute or two longer).

Melt an ounce or so of butter in a thick pan and fry off a couple of finely chopped onions in it. Add one pint of tomato juice, a tablespoonful of brown sugar, a tablespoonful of white vinegar, salt, a pinch of cayenne pepper and a hint of tabasco sauce. Pour over the cooked rabbit, cover with a lid and cook in a hot oven for about 15 minutes.

Rabbit croquettes

Mince the meat from a large tender rabbit and add an equal amount of minced beef. Add a cupful of plain boiled rice, bind with a beaten egg and season to taste. Mould into croquette shapes and fry or bake in a hot oven. If the mixture is too soft, add a little commercial packet stuffing and leave for a few minutes before shaping. The rusk content of the stuffing mix will absorb the excess moisture.

Rabbit toad in the hole

I don't really like the name but I can't think of a better one and you have my word for it that this is young rabbit at its best. Make this dish when you have to roast a big joint of prime beef and cook two meals in one.

Lay a portioned rabbit in the bottom of the roasting dish, season lightly and put the beef joint directly on top of it. Roast and baste the joint in the normal way until it is tender, then remove it from the dish.

The rabbit portions will meanwhile have absorbed much of the natural fat and juices from the beef and should be almost falling off the bones.

Two choices are now open to you.

Serve the fresh roast beef or put it away for cold cuts later.

Either way, leave the rabbit in with the beef juices. If you eat the beef there and then, set the rabbit portions, still in the roasting dish, aside for tomorrow. Re-heat it all in a hot oven and when thoroughly hot cover all with a standard Yorkshire pudding batter mixture. Bake off until the pudding has risen and is crisp.

There will almost certainly be some sticking to the bottom of the roasting dish (unless it is 100 per cent non-stick) where the juices of the beef and rabbit have mingled, but that, if anything, enhances the meal.

HARE

I have caught hares by many means which need not be discussed here, but mostly I have shot them. And in those early post-war days when the meat ration was a few pennyworth of whatever happened to be available, several pounds of hare meat was received with great rejoicing.

Hare is game in the true sense of the word. It is not highly popular in some quarters and many sportsmen give away those they shoot because they are not enamoured with the job of hanging, dressing and cooking them. Besides which, they say, hare is boring!

I do not care for the traditional procedure of hanging a hare for two weeks or so before eating it. The sight, and smell, is revolting and I really cannot understand why anyone should wish to treat meat in such a manner simply because it goes under the heading of 'game'. Why should game be improved by hanging and other meat not? Leaving the guts in a creature for weeks on end does nothing to encourage me to eat it, but I have eaten such meat and I have had experience of what has to be done.

Although there is no strict close season for killing hares, it is an offence to offer them for sale during the period between March and July (inclusive). Hares are positively better eaten in winter, which is the only time they can be traditionally hung without refrigeration.

In cold weather they may be hung outside; in damp, mild conditions they are better placed under some kind of cover, through which a cool draught of air can pass. Many large estates boast a fly-proofed game room or cage. I know of one particular grand walk-in, wire-mesh construction that catches the cool breeze and remains always in the shade of large over-hanging trees. The hares, pheasants and other game hanging inside look impressive, and his Lordship's keepers are rightly proud of both it and its contents. Me? I'd rather see all the game dressed and installed in the freezer. But who am I to argue?

A cool cellar where the air circulates freely is another good place to hang hares, and I have heard tales of trenches dug especially for that purpose, though I have not seen one in use. The hares are supposedly hung in the trench which is then covered with boards and turves until the game is required. Apart from the possibility of flies finding their way inside (which would not apply in cold weather) the idea appears sound. A covered trench ought to remain cool enough and it would be well protected from the sun. It should be remembered that even a January sun can be extremely warm on occasions.

So much for hanging hares. Then follows the ghastly business of skinning and preparing them for cooking. There is nothing difficult about skinning a hare, but the procedure is different from that of skinning a rabbit because the guts are left in. Rabbits are usually field-dressed and the guts removed for cooling and ease of carrying. Hares are hung with the guts inside, and if by chance they have been badly shot the cleaning procedure is positively revolting. Methods of removing the skin may differ from person to person and even from county to county, but it doesn't matter really how it is achieved provided the fur is kept clear of the flesh. One old-fashioned method of skinning involved the retaining of the ears which were left on during the cooking. That would be difficult for the amateur, and in any event it is completely unnecessary.

Many so-called gourmets insist that the blood should be retained for cooking and that the inside of the hare should only be wiped with a damp cloth. If that's how you like it, and if the hare has been head shot, try it. If the hare has been caught in a net or snare, again that's fine. But if half the guts have been smashed by shotgun pellets (as often happens) you will no doubt have different thoughts. Hung or not, you will almost certainly decide that washing is better than wiping, and that you can well do without that green-looking blood.

The various ways and means of cooking hares do not necessarily depend upon their being hung, so before we go on to the actual methods involved, let me tell you how I treat hare before cooking. (According to all the rules it's entirely wrong; I can only say that it tastes right.)

I treat it like a rabbit and remove the innards from the word go. Then I skin it, taking care to keep the fur off the flesh as much as possible. I feed the head, liver, kidneys and heart to the ferrets, portion the rest and wash it thoroughly several times. Then I leave it in cold salt water for several hours. After another thorough washing I soak the portions again in a bowl of ice-cold salt water (especially in mild weather) and leave it all in the refrigerator, often for as long as two days. In the process all the blood disappears; the meat becomes lighter in colour and pleasant to sight and touch. According to some, it will have lost its flavour; to me it has simply been rendered less strong (many sportsmen will not eat hare because it is regarded as 'strong').

The same salting and soaking procedure may be followed with a whole, unportioned hare, and there is no reason why the offal should not be kept and eaten if desired. I dispose of mine the way I do for reasons of simple economy and convenience.

One method of skinning a hare

Whichever way you prefer to prepare your hare, the cooking processes are more or less the same.

Jugged hare, in my opinion, tastes better when the meat has been 'de-gamed', but either way, here is a rough idea of just one simple method of preparation.

Cut all the meat from the hare and pressure cook the bones that remain with onions, carrots, mixed herbs and beef-stock cubes, to make a concentrated stock. You need about $1\frac{1}{2}$ pints to jug a regular-sized hare. Meanwhile, roll the hare meat in seasoned flour and fry off to a golden brown in hot butter.

Place the meat in a crock or stone pickle jar, cover with the stock from the pressure cooker. Add a couple of whole onions spiked with half a dozen cloves, a squeeze of lemon juice, a bay leaf, and, if you like, a glass of port or red wine. Cover the crock or jar and bake slowly at around 300°F for as long as you like. By that I mean the cooking time of approximately three hours may be exceeded or even doubled without detriment to the finished dish. Good additions to the jug are prime lean stewing beef, pearl barley, and a squeeze of tomato purée. Forcemeat stuffing balls, moulded and fried in butter, may be served with the dish on completion. Redcurrant jelly is traditionally served with hare in its many cooked forms, but if you're country bred and make crabapple jelly each year, try a little of that instead.

Roast hare is also excellent, provided the hare is young. A leveret (a young hare) is perfect. Keep the carcase whole, make a good forcemeat stuffing, adding the natural offal finely minced if desired and push the mixture well up into the breast of the hare as well as the flank cavity. Sew up with thread, place it in a baking dish, brush over with melted butter and dust very lightly with seasoned flour. Put a little concentrated stock into the baking dish, cover the hare with strips of fat pork and bake in a moderate oven. As the fat from the pork melts into the stock, baste frequently to keep it all moist. When the hare is almost cooked, remove the pork strips and continue roasting and basting frequently to brown off the hare itself.

Make a well-seasoned gravy with the juices and fats remaining in the baking dish. The crisp pieces of pork can be warmed through and softened slightly in the gravy-making process, and they should, of course, be served with the hare.

Roast hare left-overs can be made into casserole or savoury mince dishes with the addition of a little minced beef, onions and herbs. There is plenty of scope for imagination, and no reason why a pie crust should not be added, for example.

Hare pâté is delicious and can in fact be made from left-overs too. There are no strict rulings except that it should be highly seasoned, minced finely or passed through a sieve, and kept moist by the addition of butter and/or stock.

If you wish to make hare pâté in the complicated and generally recognised way, here is how to do it. In my opinion you'll be using up a lot of unnecessary time and energy (gas, electricity or whatever) and although you'll end up with a delicious product, there are easier methods of producing equally fine pâté.

Line a casserole dish with thick bacon slices, place hare portions on top and press down tightly. Add bay leaves, seasoning and a little garlic salt. Cover with more bacon slices, pour in a little stock and allow it to soak into the packed meat. Bake in a slow oven for 3 or 4 hours, moistening with stock occasionally if necessary. When thoroughly cooked, remove the bones and pass all the remaining meat through a fine mincer twice.

Season highly to taste and pass all the mixture through a medium sieve. For storing, place in small jars and cover with clarified butter.

A much simpler method, and one that gives scope for more imagination, is outlined in the Pigeon chapter. That simple procedure can, with all kinds of additions, produce a fine rough pâté from any edible game - any mixture of game, or any mixture of game, wild fowl and vermin. All it takes is imagination! (A 'mixed-game' pâté is described in the More Mixed Dishes chapter.)

Has anyone heard of hare sausage, I wonder? If not, allow me to recommend those made at our house.

Soak about ½ lb of stale bread and squeeze it out as dry as . possible. Mix it together with ½ lb finely minced fat beef and an equal amount of finely minced hare. Add salt, black pepper, sage, thyme or mixed herbs (be a little heavy on the pepper) and mould the mixture into thin croquette shapes. If the mixture is too moist, dry it off with a little bread crumb.

Variations on the basic sausage mixture are endless, and depend largely on the seasonings used, but a few hints regarding the actual texture of the mixture may be worth recording here. If raw hare meat is used it is possible that the mixture will be too soft. Its 'mushy' texture can be improved by steam-cooking the hare portions slightly first. This firms up the meat considerably, and when mixed with the raw beef it should be nice and workable.

Some soft mixtures will benefit from the addition of a couple of raw eggs which will help the binding process. Such soft mixtures can actually be piped through a savoy bag with a plain tube attachment. They are especially good for making sausage rolls in bulk.

Firm basic mixtures can be turned from sausage to meat ball, croquette, rissole or cutlet shapes and altered in flavour by the addition of finely chopped onions, shallots or chives. The can be baked off 'hash' style, made into savoury pies, pasties or turnovers, and they can be fried in their various shapes. They can be made into snacks or main meals and served hot or cold with salads, vegetables or pickles.

I could go on, and more specific hare recipes follow, but in the meantime consider for a moment the many other ways in which hare might be used to extend and improve other meat dishes. Who said it was boring?

SOME MORE HARE RECIPES

Hare Casserole

Portion the hare and place as many of the pieces as required into a casserole dish. Fry off diced onions, carrots and celery in hot butter or fat, dust with flour and cook until brown. Place vegetables on top of the hare portions, cover with well seasoned stock, add sliced tomatoes, a little chopped green pepper and a pinch of mixed herbs. Cook slowly in a covered dish until the gravy is thick and meat is falling off the bones. Adjust the seasoning and serve.

Left-overs, when cold, can be separated from the bones, packed into waxed cartons and deep frozen for future quick meals.

Barbecued Hare

First make a barbecue sauce from lemon juice, butter, tomato ketchup, brown sugar, salt, pepper, tabasco sauce, and a little dry mustard. You need about equal amounts of butter and ketchup (say about 4 tablespoons of each), melt both together, thin down with about the same quantity of lemon juice (half and half vinegar and lemon juice will also be suitable). Add the seasonings and simmer all together for about 15 minutes with the lid off the pan. This will reduce the liquid slightly.

Brush the hare portions with the sauce and grill for half and hour or so, brushing with sauce frequently. Alternatively, wrap the hare portions (covered liberally with the sauce) into a foil pack and bake for 1 ½ hours in a hot oven.

There are of course many ways of varying the sauce, and hare can also be prepared in any of the cook-in sauces mentioned at the beginning of this book.

Curried Hare

Prepare the hare as for jugging. Pressure cook bones, etc. to make a concentrated stock. Fry off hare portions with diced onions and carrots, dust with flour and curry powder and place all in a casserole dish.

Cover with concentrated stock, season with salt, pepper, and any favourite herbs and spices. Add sultanas, sliced apple, dessicated coconut, chutney, English or French mustard, and a little tomato ketchup. Cook in a slow oven with a lid on the casserole dish until tender, and serve with plain boiled rice.

VENISON

I HAVE ONLY EVER killed two deer in my life. On both occasions it was an act of mercy, because the animals had been hit by vehicles and were lying there with broken limbs, unable to move. I have never had any qualms about killing rabbits, game, turkeys and poultry, and I pride myself that I can do so as effectively as anyone and better than most. But to have to kill a 200 lb buck with a fillet knife (as I did once in Illinois at 3 o'clock in the morning), and to have to dispatch a roe deer in Hampshire with a sharp penknife at about the same hour in the morning, were jobs I would have preferred not to do. But I was glad, at least, that I was there and able to summon up the will to do it. What would have been the fate of those animals if some kindly old lady had been driving the cars concerned? How many would know just where to place the blade and pierce the jugular to bring about instant death? I'm not trying to make myself appear smart; I'm just wondering how many other deer have met the same fate *without* being despatched quickly and humanely.

But while sentiment played its part at the time, I saw no virtue in leaving those carcases for dogs or carrion crows and, legally or not, I picked them up and moved on with them.

I know that deer should be paunched quickly and dressed out as soon as possible after being killed. I know my American friends do not waste time over this chore and, although I lack expertise at dealing with deer, I came out of it on both occasions with no feeling of shame. I hung my deer up by the two front feet, and paunched and skinned them on the spot.

The big buck was butchered the same day and, not knowing anything about it but having butchered pigs before, I did it the only way I knew how. It wasn't right, but it worked and there was no waste. The smaller deer I washed in the chalk stream with the help of the keeper to whom I reported the incident. He dressed and butchered it properly for me and took a haunch for his reward. Those are the only two whole animals I have been associated with, and any other knowledge of this particular kind of cookery has been acquired as a result of friends bearing gifts of venison.

The tenderloin portion that lies along the backbone below the chest cavity is by far and away the most sought-after portion. Like fillet steak or pork fillet it is always sweet, always tender and needs only a few minutes' cooking. Cut against the grain it makes small cutlets, but they are infinitely more succulent than if the fillet is cut lengthwise. You may grill, broil, charcoal, barbecue or hot fry these tenderloin portions.

They'll melt in your mouth whichever way you cook them, but *please* use only quick-cooking methods. To stew or casserole such meat is sacrilegious!

The haunch is reputed to be the prime roasting portion and provided it has sufficient fat to permit roasting without drying, it is indeed a tasty cut. Doe meat is reputed to be of lower quality than that of the buck, but I am no connoisseur so I cannot comment. I know that in cold weather a haunch of venison tastes better if it is hung for a week or so. It needs regular inspection for tainting even then, and if you can persuade your butcher to hang it in his cold room you will have no problems.

The same applies, of course, to all other cuts of venison. It is not recommended, generally speaking, that venison should be eaten at once. An interesting point comes to light here, however, and I mention it because I believe it is relevant.

I have put venison into deep freeze the day after it was killed and, with no thought of hanging in mind, I have cooked it after defrosting some weeks later. It was delicious and I wonder if the deep freezing process affected the flesh in a manner similar to that brought about by hanging? (I have a friend who deep freezes his pheasants whole and firmly insists that they are much better than those hung traditionally.)

I do not like the thought of putting unprepared game into my freezer but I have always believed firmly in processing all my fish, game, meat or poultry for the deep freeze with as little time lag as possible. So it has been with venison and I have no complaints. Traditional recipes for the roasting of a haunch of venison call for marinading in oil, herbs and vinegar, but this is not strictly necessary.

Roast it as you would a leg of lamb, adding fat or butter and basting frequently if the meat is dry. Serve with a rich brown gravy and redcurrant jelly.

The truth is that you can treat venison in pretty much the same way as you would treat beef. Some cuts will roast, some will grill, some will fry, and some will have to be stewed, minced or casseroled. Shoulder cuts can be treated in the same way as the haunch.

Chops or cutlets can be cooked as you would cook lamb chops. The neck *can* be roasted but it is better, I think, cooked in a casserole. Trimmings can be used for 'deerburgers' or rissoles, and heart, liver and kidneys can be treated like any other kind of offal.

Venison meat loaf is popular in certain parts of North America and the following recipe given to me in Minnesota was reputed to be of early Indian origin. I make no claims except that it tastes excellent. Here is how it is made.

Mince together about 2 lb of venison and $\frac{1}{2}$ lb of pork, and fry gently together. Stir in 4 tablespoons of flour and a $\frac{1}{2}$ pint measure of dry breadcrumbs. Add a small finely chopped onion and some chopped parsley. Season with salt and pepper, soften with a little milk and mix well. Mould into loaf shape, place in a suitable tin and bake off slowly at 350°F. Carve when cold.

In recent years the small muntjac deer has multiplied in many areas to the extent that it is now becoming a problem. I am not 'into' hunting muntjac deer, but when keeper friends have to consider culling, I ask them always to consider me!

In the past these small deer featured only rarely in our household but they were always regarded as a delicacy when they did. In recent years I have had more opportunity to dress out and prepare muntjac venison and, the more I do so, the more I am inclined to compare it with the meat of kangaroo.

This is really no place to discuss the delights of 'roo meat but it has to be said that my experiences in the Australian bush, where I have often 'survived' on 'roo, rabbit and wild duck of various kinds, have taught me how to deal with our own muntjac.

It has to be said that the meat of both creatures is almost completely free of fat and that provision for some kind of 'dripping agent' has to be made to prevent dryness when roasting, grilling or barbecuing. Today it is regarded as almost obscene to talk of using animal fat of any kind, for it would appear that such practice will have us all in our graves in next to no time. I believe, however, that we all need a certain amount of fat. I also believe that there is sweet reason in using enough but not too much.

The old-fashioned procedure known as 'larding' will improve over lean meat beyond belief. It is a chore I do not particularly relish, but I cannot deny its value. Narrow strips of bacon (you can use fresh pork) cut from rashers and referred to as 'lardoons' are literally stitched into the joint of meat with a large sacking needle. It is possible to work the lardoon in and out several times when all goes well but for the most part a 2" lardoon, inserted so that both ends are exposed, is good enough. I stress that it is not strictly necessary to lard venison but I have been pleased with the results of doing so. Muntjac is nevertheless excellent roasted slowly on a bed of bones and covered with strips of belly pork.

The following are recipes for various deer given to me by friends in the U.S.A. where deer are harvested in thousands every year. Any of them may be applied to our own deer species including muntjac.

Chops

8 venison chops
2 large onions (sliced)
2 large mushrooms (sliced)
1 can mushroom soup (concentrated)
$\frac{1}{4}$ teaspoon tabasco sauce
1 measure sherry
$\frac{1}{4}$ lb. butter
$\frac{1}{4}$ pt. water.
Salt, pepper.
Fry off onions and mushrooms.
Fry off chops in same fat.
Place chops in dish and cover with other ingredients thoroughly mixed. Bake in covered dish for 40 minutes then remove cover for a further 10 minutes.
Serve with brown rice and sweet peppers.

Steaks

4 medium venison steaks
1 lb. sausage meat
2 large mushrooms, finely chopped
1 large onion, finely chopped
1 egg
2 tablespoons of uncooked rice
1 half-bottle of burgundy.
Salt, pepper.

Place 2 of the steaks in non-stick casserole. Mix all other solid ingredients and spread over the steaks. Place the remaining steaks on top and cover again with remaining mixture. Pour on the wine. Cover and bake slowly for $2\frac{1}{2}$ -3 hours.

Roast
　　1 roasting joint of venison
　　$\frac{1}{2}$ pt. apple juice
　　1 large cooking apple (sliced)
　　1 large onion (sliced)
　　1 stick celery (chopped)
　　1 tablespoon flour
　　Salt and pepper.
　　Place roast in dish. Smother with chopped vegetables. Stir flour into apple juice. Pour over and cook slowly until tender.

Sausage
　　2 lb. minced venison
　　$\frac{3}{4}$ lb. minced smoked ham
　　$\frac{1}{4}$ lb. minced fat bacon
　　1 teaspoon mixed herbs
　　1 teaspoon pepper
　　1 teaspoon salt
　　1 pinch chilli pepper (optional)
　　1 egg
　　$\frac{1}{4}$ lb. breadcrumbs (or more if needed to dry off mixture). Mix all ingredients together (by hand or slow speed mixer). Adjust seasoning and cook as burgers, patties, or croquettes. Surplus may be wrapped in film and deep-frozen in raw state.

Marinade
　　1 tin tomatoes (passed through sieve)
　　$\frac{1}{2}$ cup honey
　　4 'shots' of bourbon
　　1 chopped onion

¼ cup soy sauce

¼ teaspoon ground ginger

Marinade roast joint for 24 hours, turning frequently. Place in roasting dish, cover with thick bacon slices and roast slowly, adding marinade and basting often.

Stir 2 tablespoons of flour into residue sauce and add two glasses of red wine. Place joint back in dish. Strain sauce through sieve over joint and re-heat.

'Porcupine'

I have to say that this is a follow-up from another recipe which bears no resemblance to it. The use of toothpicks led me to dream up the following roast. The principle may be applied to any lean joint, whether marinated in advance or not.

Place joint in roasting dish. Stick toothpicks liberally into it and on each toothpick impale a small pickling onion and a chunky cube of belly pork before roasting. The spiked portions will be cooked first, of course, but may be treated as hors d'oeuvre.

And, finally, here is a thought for the future. It has to do with a kangaroo leg recipe I once tried in the outback. It was cooked in a Dutch camp oven and declared to be perfect by all concerned. I have *not* cooked venison this way as yet, but I am *positive* it cannot fail to be delicious.

Cut several deep slits into a haunch (not boned) and stuff them full of forcemeat stuffing made as described earlier but containing a liberal quantity of finely chopped fat bacon (or pork) and a squirt of tomato puree. Roast in the normal style and baste frequently.

SQUIRREL

I FIRST TASTED squirrel in the USA back in 1967. I was staying with friends in Illinois and they, knowing me to be interested in cooking, asked me to 'fix an English style rabbit pie' with rabbit from the freezer.

I remarked, as I prepared the portions, that some of the rabbits were small. 'They are squirrels,' said my host. 'I mix 'em up. They taste the same - sometimes a little better'.

I cooked them rabbit style, and, with a certain amount of apprehension, served them to the families present. The meal was pronounced a great success and, although I hesitated at first, I found myself eating and enjoying what was, in effect, squirrel and rabbit pie.

In the USA squirrels are considered to be prime game. A season and a bag limit are imposed and squirrel are hunted with both rifle and shotgun.

In Britain, we shoot squirrels only when we encounter them in the woods while seeking other game. We do not hunt them; for some reason we do not recognise them as food and those we shoot are seldom taken away. The tails may be removed for future fly-tying but the meat is usually left to rot, which is a shocking waste of good food.

Squirrels live on the best of food themselves. They eat nuts and grain for most of the time and most people would agree that 'corn-fed' meat is top grade. Which means, generally speaking, that squirrel tastes better than rabbit. If you can overcome the prejudice that stems from the fact that they are often referred to as 'tree rats' you will find grey squirrel to be excellent game. The carcase needs little in the way of field treatment. Obviously it should be kept cool and, in warm weather such as we often experience during October, it should not be hung where flies can blow it.

Squirrels can he paunched in the field just like rabbits, but if this is done it tends to make the skinning a little difficult back at base. They *can* be skinned like rabbits after gutting, but there is a better way of doing it. By cutting around the under-side of the tail and, with a very sharp knife, bringing two skin cuts around each side of the body to meet in the middle of the chest, the squirrel can be skinned in two operations. The first pull is on the tail. Holding the back legs in one hand (or standing on them if the going is tough) pull on the tail and take off the portion of skin that includes the front legs and head. Then, holding the tail which is now hanging over the head end, pull on that pointed portion of the skin over the chest cavity. That will remove the half which includes the rear legs. At this point the skin, head and front feet can be cut off to release the forward half of the skin and the back feet can be cut to release the rear portion.

We now have a skinned squirrel with the intestines still intact and these should be removed. This kind of operation can be carried out in the field. It is, in fact, advisable in warm weather, and, if the meat is wrapped in a piece of cheesecloth carried for the purpose, it will remain in excellent condition until it can be cleaned off properly.

Washed in cold water (a little salt if the animal is badly shot) it can be cooked the following day or consigned to the freezer.

Young squirrels can be fried. They are as sweet as the nuts they eat and if rolled in seasoned flour and cooked slowly with thick streaky pork or bacon rashers there is no meat more tasty.

They may be stuffed and roasted in exactly the same way as rabbits and with the same dressing. And of course they can be braised, stewed or made into pies. In each case the rabbit 'recipe' may be followed.

Two dishes, a little out of the ordinary, but very easy to prepare, are squirrel with brown dumplings and squirrel beans.

Squirrel with brown dumplings

Fry off the squirrel portions in shallow fat until brown. Remove and set them in a deep baking dish. Fry off diced carrots, onions and celery (to taste). Dust with flour and continue cooking until the flour browns. Remove pan from the heat, stir in boiling stock (made from a chicken cube) and season.

Pour the thickened stock over the meat portions, and bring it all back to boiling point.

Make a dumpling dough with self-raising flour, salt, lard or white fat in the proportion of 4 oz fat to 1 lb flour, and sufficient water to make a stiff dough. Mould the dumplings, place them into the boiling stock and push them under.

Place the dish in a moderate oven, leave the lid off, and cook slowly until the meat is tender and the dumplings are crisp and brown. Submerging them completely ensures a crisp, brown finish and enhances their taste.

Squirrel beans

Dice and fry off several rashers of fatty bacon and remove them from the pan. Fry off some squirrel portions in the fat that remains.

Cook slowly, with the lid on the pan, *until tender*. Remove the portions and place them in the dish with the bacon. Fry off one large onion chopped small and add it to the bacon and squirrel. Open one tin of baked beans, stir into them about an eggcupful of vinegar and a dessertspoonful of brown sugar. Thin down with water or stock, pour over meat, bacon and onions, bring to the boil and simmer for about 5 minutes. Add the final seasoning at this stage.

There is no end to the possibilities. Squirrel needs no camouflaging or enhancing. The meat is white and sweet and may safely be cooked in all traditional styles.

The following is a traditional recipe from the middle west of the USA and you have my word for it that it is excellent.

Squirrel stew

Cook the squirrel portions in salted water or stock for about an hour and add chopped onions and carrots while they are still cooking. When the portions are tender add half a tin of tomato juice, a few thinly sliced mushrooms, a diced green pepper, a little canned sweetcorn (or fresh if available), a pinch of sage and a liberal shake of black pepper.

With vegetable oil and flour (about 1 tablespoonful of each) make a white roux and thicken the stew. Bring it back to the boil, remove from the heat and stir in a liberal helping of fresh cream.

The dish can be changed but not necessarily improved by placing it in a casserole dish, covering the top with grated cheese and browning under the grill. It is not a dish for the weight-conscious, but as it is very filling, a small portion is very often sufficient for a hungry man.

PHEASANT

IF YOU WANT pheasant to serve as game in the truest sense of word, that is to say well hung and 'high', bear a few points in mind. It doesn't worry me whether you do it rightly or wrongly -I've already made my personal feelings quite clear on high game of any kind, but I've also seen plenty of so-called game that I would not offer to my ferrets for fear of offending them!

If a pheasant has been shot, injured, caught by a dog and finally despatched by the shooter, there's more than an even chance, in my experience, that the bird will end up by having its neck wrung. And that means it's no longer 'game'. Experienced keepers know just how to tap a bird on the head with a stick, and in my father's day game rings were commonplace. They housed a long spike which was pushed into the brain of the bird, killing it instantly. Another way of despatching an injured pheasant, and one which I invariably practice myself, is to crack its head like a nut between my teeth. It

44

sounds ghastly, and it may appear uncivilised, but it keeps the bird whole and leaves a strong neck which will carry it safely on a regular game stringer. Game birds are carried feet downwards and not held by the feet like freshly killed hens.

Birds with necks that have been broken hang by a mere thread of skin when placed on the stringer. That skin grows longer and longer until the birds resemble vultures rather than pheasants, and almost invariably lose their heads before the end of the day. Offering a guest, a housewife or a syndicate member a beheaded pheasant with a protruding neck bone covered in dried blood and feathers is an embarrassing business. Keep pheasant necks whole at all times. Don't imagine the smart thing to do is to hold the head and swing the bird round in a circle until the neck gives. It only looks smart to those who know no better. Pheasants are usually hung by their necks for as long a period as is deemed necessary by those who are about to eat them but I am told on good authority by a keeper to one of the country's largest estates that a better way is to lay them on their backs on a narrow bench. That way the breast cavity remains clear and the entrails literally dry out on the lower half of the back. *That*, he assured me, would change my opinion of hung game because *that* is the *correct* way. I make no claims. I have not tried it. I have not seen it carried out that way, but I am prepared to believe he was telling me the truth.

It has been my duty on many occasions to cook high game for others to eat, so please do not think this chapter will deal with game only as I like it. Pheasant can taste pleasant; it can also taste like cartwheel grease. I don't believe age has anything to do with it. Having experienced the same problem with rabbit and duck over the years, I'm almost convinced that it stems from the bird's diet. Anyone who has eaten rabbit killed in a turnip field will have some idea of what I mean.

Fred Buller, a friend, traveller and excellent game shot (on occasions) told me many years ago that the way to ensure the removal of any doubtful taste is to skin the bird rather than pluck it. For many years, on and off, I have skinned my birds to save time and inconvenience. At the end of a long day's shoot, and with thoughts of an early morning start next day, skinning has proved to be a very practical solution. My birds are in the freezer the day they are shot (almost as fast as Mr Birdseye's peas). For special meals and dinner parties, my birds were always plucked for the part, but Fred Buller's advice drew my attention to the fact that none of my skinned birds had ever been other than excellent. Now *all* my birds are skinned. The wings are clipped off with secateurs and fed, with other oddments, to the ferrets. Pheasant wings are the hardest part of the bird to prepare and offer the least meat. They're not worth the effort. With wings, head and legs removed it's easy to split open the skin at the breast bone and peel it all off in one piece with scarcely a feather out of place.

Fred Buller's theory (and he is simply repeating advice given to him) is that the fat layer between the skin and the flesh of the bird is the cause of the trouble. Get rid of that and your bird will be wholesome. I believe it because he has been proved right so many, many times.

Some shooters and gourmets have raised their hands in horror when I've suggested it. You cannot roast a skinned pheasant, they've wailed. All I can say is they should taste it the way my wife does it.

She cuts the bird up the middle to make two equal portions, brushes each with oil, butter or pork lard, sprinkles lightly with flour, salt, pepper and mixed herbs. She covers the whole thing with thick rashers of streaky pork and roasts until the pork is crisp. Then she removes the pork and bastes continually with the deep juices that have dripped out of the meat. She turns the bird portions several times so that the breast meat softens in the juice.

Occasionally she will fill the breast cavities with a good forcemeat stuffing. Excess fat is poured off once the bird portions are cooked and the brown residue in the dish is used to make a rich gravy. This is especially good if thickened with a brown roux.

If one pheasant has to serve four people, it is advisable to cut the portions before cooking. It makes the dish easier to serve and allows for better cooking control.

But roast pheasant is only one dish. A nice dish it's true, but far from being the best. There are scores of others which take less time and are equally palatable.

Pheasant cutlets, for example, take a little longer to prepare, but are very quick to cook. A young hen bird is preferable to a cock. Divide the bird into joints and remove the bones from each portion with a sharp fillet knife. Flatten each piece and firm into a good shape. Roll in seasoned flour, dip in beaten egg, roll in breadcrumbs and fry gently in hot fat.

Pressure-cook bones and remnants to make a concentrated stock, and from this make the light or dark sauce of your choice to serve with the cutlets. Removing all the bones is not essential but in my opinion it improves the dish.

Pheasant and brown rice is a favourite dish prepared by my wife, usually from left-over pheasant. I prefer it if the pheasant is raw to begin with, but left-over cooked breasts are excellent.

Fry together some finely chopped bacon, sliced onion and finely chopped pheasant. Add some finely chopped mushrooms and a little celery (optional). Bring to the boil some brown rice and cook until tender. Refresh under a cold tap, strain and tip in with the chopped meat mixture. Season well with, cayenne pepper, salt and a little Worcestershire sauce, turn up the heat and stir with a wooden spatula until all is piping hot. Garnish with a little parsley and serve with crusty bread and butter. Don't spoil this dish by serving vegetables or potatoes - it 's good enough on its own.

Left-over pheasant can be made into a different kind of croquette by the following method. Mince finely all available left-overs. Add some chicken, veal or other meat if you need to increase the bulk. Moisten it all with a little thick, brown sauce, crack in a couple of eggs, salt, pepper, seasoning and a few breadcrumbs. Stir all the ingredients together while warming gently over a low heat. When the mixture thickens, tip out on to a floured tray and flatten. Cut or mould into rounds, coat with egg and breadcrumb, and fry in hot shallow fat until nicely browned.

Hot pheasant pie may he prepared in the same fashion as rabbit or rook pie. It makes little difference whether the sauce or gravy is white or brown but traditionally it should, perhaps, be white and enriched with a little full cream.

And, of course, pheasant left-overs can quickly be made into delicious little snack-meal vol-au-vents.

Use the puff pastry mix described earlier, roll out to about 5/8 in. thick and cut into rounds with an appropriate cutter. Using a smaller cutter, *half* cut through the centre of the round and withdraw the tool. Bake these cases off at 425°F (leave in a warm room for at least 20 minutes after traying and before baking to ensure evenly shaped cases).

Finely chop left-over pheasant meat (add a little left-over forcemeat if available) and mix into a *thick*, white, well-seasoned sauce.

When the cases are baked, remove the lids formed by the second cutting with the smaller tool. These will have risen to above the level of the main case. Scrape out the middle of the case and fill with the pheasant/sauce mixture (which I emphasise must be stiff), and garnish the top with a tiny leaf of parsley which should be left showing when the lid is replaced. This pheasant/sauce mixture can be flavoured with a little salad cream if desired. It can be enriched with thick cream, and it can be extended with chopped button mushrooms. Once more, I will make the point that there is no end to the theme, and it is wide open to imagination. The same mixture, tightened with a little breadcrumb, some extra minced meat, a finely chopped raw potato and a diced onion, can be used as a filling for pasties or plate pies. And, as we shall see, there are many ways of mixing game and other meats to make dishes that are both tasty and economical.

Traditionally hung pheasants are usually roasted. They may he stuffed with minced beef, covered with sliced fat bacon, roasted and basted frequently with melted butter. When almost cooked the bacon may be removed and the breast of the bird dusted with flour and basted frequently to give a nut-brown colour.

Strictly speaking the minced beef should not be served with the pheasant (but who's looking?) and the traditional extras are bread sauce and fried breadcrumbs which are served in separate dishes.

The following recipe for pheasant was passed on to me recently by a close friend. He calls it the 'Docs' Recipe' because the two doctors who recommend it are man and wife and both Cordon Bleu cooks.

Take pair of secateurs, cut off neck, head, wings and legs. Skin out with scalpel. Cover with streaky bacon. Put the bird in the oven preheated to 500°F and cook for 45 min. Fifteen minutes before end of the cooking time, pour $\frac{1}{4}$ pint of strong cider over bird and baste frequently.

In recent years driven pheasant shoots have become more and more popular, with the result that pheasants have become decidedly undervalued. For several seasons I have been able to buy end-of-shoot birds at £2.00 per brace. What the future holds is anyone's guess but, until the average housewife begins to appreciate the true value of a brace of birds (in terms of meat for the table), I expect pheasant to remain cheap. That suits me. I shoot a few myself but I also see the economic sense of ordering about 20 brace during the shooting season.

I find it hard to understand folk who profess not to like pheasant but who have eaten it with relish when I have served it. I find it equally hard to understand why so many housewives (or their doting husbands) recoil with horror at the thought of plucking and/or dressing out a pheasant. They accept that £2.00 a brace is excellent value but in many cases they expect them to be oven-ready!

The simple skinning method, as described earlier, requires no scalpel nor does it really require secateurs. A sharp chopping knife will cut off wings, head and legs as described, and the skinning can be carried out without any other instruments. It is a foolproof method and after the guts have been removed, the carcase can be washed thoroughly under a cold tap. I have, on many occasions, skinned, cleaned, portioned and bagged as many as 20 brace of birds in a morning. My method wastes nothing whatsoever since the heads and wings are saved for ferret fodder and the neck and giblets are retained for stock.

There is no point in attempting to salvage meat from wings. It is more trouble than it is worth. And here is a point worthy of consideration. When presented with a freshly skinned and gutted pheasant, it really does make sense to cut out the whole of the backbone entirely. Take off the legs with a sharp knife, remove the breast on the bone from the backbone (here's where secateurs really come in handy) and then freezer pack it all with the two legs nestling in the breastbone cavity.

It will take up about half the freezer room of a whole bird and the backbone remainders can be pressure cooked along with the giblets to make a stock which may be stored in the freezer until needed. When I have had a large number of birds to prepare, I store the game stock in large, plastic, screw-topped mineral water bottles (about two-thirds filled). At some later date, with more game, rabbit or wildfowl bones to process, I use this frozen stock instead of water. I often repeat this process several times and you have my word for it that the resulting concentrated stock has to be tasted to be believed. I have often taken several quarts of it, made into prime game soup, on winter fishing parties, and I have never known any to be left.

When pheasants are really cheap (I regard £2.00 per brace as cheap and am happy to pay £3.00 per brace, but I have heard of gamekeepers being unable to give birds away at the end of shoots!), it is time to experiment and dream up new dishes. Most pheasants are young, tender birds (those that are old are usually recognisable) and in recent years I have taken to filleting out the two breast portions and frying them in shallow fat after dusting with seasoned flour. It is simple and not wasteful since the bones (again) are used for stock. These fillets are especially tasty cooked on a plate- (not grille) type barbecue unit.

A particular favourite with my friends and family has not yet been given a name. It is tedious to prepare but very convenient to serve. The breasts are cut and/or sliced into portions to suit individual tastes and two of these portions are sandwiched together with a spoonful or so of moist stuffing or forcemeat. These are then rolled and wrapped with very thinly cut streaky bacon, packed *tightly* into a square or oblong baking dish, covered with foil and baked in a hot oven. Timing is very elastic to suit the size of the portions. Once cooked the 'parcels' hold their shape and may be served piled on a platter or whatever.

It is not always easy to acquire very thin rashers but I regard them as essential. A friendly bacon shop proprietor provides me with a whole flank which has been boned, skinned, sliced and wrapped. I use the discarded skin for 'crackling' and the bones for whatever takes my fancy.

Wrapping the 'parcels' takes time and patience but I find it easy enough to organise a production line. Handling two layers of meat and a soft stuffing centre requires a certain amount of manipulation and yet the whole process can be undertaken very quickly if a few simple steps are followed.

1. Lay two rashers horizontally edge to edge.
2. Lay two more vertically on top of them to form a cross.
3. Place first layer of pheasant at the intersection.
4. Cover with forcemeat.
5. Place second layer on top of forcemeat.
6. Fold edges of all four rashers over the sandwich and make up the 'parcel'.

From then on the portions are easy to handle and pack for cooking. Any left over will, if chilled in the refrigerator, carve into very attractive, thin round slices to serve with salad or as sandwich fillings.

At this point it suddenly occurs to me that we might decide to call this dish 'Pheasant Parcels'. Why not?

Its early success has led me to use pigeon breasts and boned-out rabbit portions in exactly the same way. Both, or even a mixture of all three, may be similarly processed and results are guaranteed.

PARTRIDGE AND GROUSE

I KNOW THESE are two entirely different birds but from the culinary point of view they may be treated in much the same way. To deal with them in two separate chapters would entail repetition and my own experience with both species is somewhat limited anyway.

Our own partridge is, today, a much less common bird than it was in pre-insecticide days. The red-legged partridge (or Frenchman as it is often called by field sportsmen) has to some extent replaced our native bird.

Both kinds are reared and planted by the fraternity but extensive stocking programmes seldom do much to increase the numbers of birds per acre. It is a put-and-take operation and annual returns are fairly predictable. Meanwhile each territory holding stocks of wild birds continues to produce roughly the same number of coveys each season. Breeders are now producing a 'hybrid' grey partridge X red-legged partridge in the hope of retaining larger numbers of resident birds. In the main I think it is fair to say that, although in many areas the partridge remains a rare bird and an absolute table luxury, the sport of shooting has ensured its survival.

Grouse inhabit an entirely different kind of territory, of course. Unlike the partridge, which is to be found in good, well-tended farm land, grouse are creatures of the wild untamed moors and heaths. Their conservation is of great importance to the shooting gentry and the ritual of haste, the rushing of the first birds killed on opening day to distant restaurants, and the serving of those birds cooked on the evening of the same day, is still observed in many quarters where expense is no object. Such a ritual is not, to the best of my knowledge, applied to the season's first partridge drive.

I have already expressed my disapproval with regard to the lengthy hanging of game, but I feel just as strongly about eating it 'warm'. By which, of course, I mean that a certain amount of time should be allowed between the killing and cooking of all game birds.

I believe that grouse and partridge need 24 hours, but I to add that it is purely a personal opinion. If gourmets like to leave partridge for several days, or eat grouse almost before they have cooled off, that is their business. I do not believe the average shooting man and his wife wish to be so precise, nor do I believe that they enjoy their game any the less for it.

Having said that grouse and partridge may be regarded as similar birds from a culinary point of view, let me now prove it to some extent by giving two recipes from a very old cookery book. It belonged, I believe, to my great-grandmother, it is dog-eared and nondescript in appearance, but its contents have been proved beyond any doubt through several generations.

Roasted Grouse

Two grouse, two slices of toast, butter, brown gravy, bread sauce, fried breadcrumbs and bacon.

Allow the birds to hang for 3-4 days in a cool place. Pluck and draw them as for roast chicken. Tie over each breast a thin slice of bacon and roast for 35 minutes in a moderate heat, basting with butter occasionally to prevent dryness. When nearly cooked, remove the bacon, dust birds with flour and baste again to make them brown. Toast the bread, and when the birds are just over half-cooked, place a slice under each one to catch the drippings. Serve the birds on the toast with bread sauce, gravy and breadcrumbs in separate dishes.

Roasted Partridge

One partridge, brown gravy, bread sauce, fried breadcrumbs, a slice of toast, butter for basting and a slice of bacon.

Pluck and draw as for roast chicken. Cover the breast with a slice of bacon and roast in a moderate oven for 30 minutes, basting frequently with hot butter.

Ten minutes before serving, remove the bacon, dust the bird with flour and baste again to give a light brown colour. Dip toast into the drippings, place bird on top and serve with gravy, bread sauce and fried breadcrumbs separately.

Apart from a five minute time difference (which means nothing because timing can only be appropriate), and a slight difference in wording, recipe number two is simply recipe number one cut in half. I have tried partridge and grouse many times (partridge more often than grouse because of accessibility) and there is no doubt in my mind that the one recipe will do for both birds. So too will the recipes that follow, despite their titles. And on reflection, is there any reason why, with cooking time adjustments, these same recipes could not be applied to pigeon, pheasant, snipe, woodcock, even rabbit? Of course not. As I have said so many times, cooking game does not need a scientific approach. Common sense is the most important ingredient.

GROUSE AND PARTRIDGE RECIPES

Grouse Pie

One brace of grouse, 3 thick rashers of bacon, ½ pint of stock, 1 lb of good beef steak, 2 hard-boiled eggs, seasoning, puff pastry.

Cut the birds into portions, cutting out the back bone completely with secateurs or a heavy-duty chopping knife. Cut bacon and steak into cubes and the eggs into slices. Line the pie dish with half of the beef and bacon, cover with grouse and top up with sliced egg and the meat and bacon remainder. Add stock, cover with pastry crust and bake for 20 minutes in a hot oven (425°F) to make the pastry rise. Lower heat to 325°F and continue cooking slowly for another $1\frac{1}{2}$ hours. Brush pastry with beaten egg 20 minutes before removing from the oven. If the pastry takes on too dark a colour, cover with a sheet of foil or brown paper and use the lowest oven shelf to provide bottom heat only.

Make a rich gravy with the giblets, neck and trimmings and pour into the pie before serving. Onions, carrots, mushrooms and mixed herbs may be added to the meat in the initial stages to provide a different flavour and 'stretch' the portions.

Partridge in Aspic

One cold cooked partridge (removed from bones and chopped), 3 hard-boiled eggs, 1 lb chopped cooked ham, aspic jelly (made with seasoned stock and gelatine according to maker's directions. These vary somewhat and it is important to follow them correctly).

The simplest method of preparation is to *fill* a jelly mould with the mixed meats and egg portions, pour in the cooling aspic and allow all to set in a refrigerator before turning out to serve. By pouring a little aspic into the mould and 'swirling' it around until it sets in a thin, all-round layer, however, a basis for decoration can be established. Shaped pieces of ham and egg can then be pressed into the sides and bottom to serve as an 'outer cover'. Fill the remaining mould with the chopped partridge meat and top up with aspic jelly gradually, an inch at a time, allowing each inch to set firmly before adding the next.

Partridge Purée

Left-over partridge meat, clear stock, butter, full cream, and seasoning.

Pass the meat through a fine mincer several times, moistening continually with stock and melted butter. Pass through a soup sieve, stir in thick cream and season to taste. Serve on hot, buttered toast to make a little go a long way.

Broiled Grouse

One grouse, butter, cayenne pepper, salt.

Cut the bird (it must be young and tender) in half length-wise and flatten between two chopping boards.

Brush with warm butter, season and place under a hot grill. Continue grilling and brushing with butter until cooked. Serve with a mushroom sauce or one of the barbecue or cook-in sauces already described. If the bird portions are brushed alternately with butter *and* barbecue sauce the flavour will be noticeably different (though not necessarily better).

Larded Partridge (English Style, according to an American friend who gave me the recipe).

Three partridge, fat pork or bacon, melted butter, half a cup of cooking sherry, watercress and toast.

Stuff the birds with traditional sage and onion stuffing, 'lard' them with strips of pork or bacon, place in a casserole dish and bake uncovered for 20 minutes, basting well with butter several times. Pour over the sherry, reduce heat to 325°F, cover the dish and cook until all is tender.

Ten minutes before serving, remove the lid to let the uncovered portions brown off. Cover a large oval plate with slices of toast, arrange the birds, garnish with watercress and serve with a suitably flavoured sauce, which may be made from the liquid after skimming off the surplus fat.

Breast of Grouse Chasseur (This is another dish from America which is also used for chukkar - a bird similar, I believe, to our red-legged partridge).

Two grouse, seasoning, celery, parsley, onion, carrot, bay leaf, 3 oz flour, one tin of tomatoes, lemon juice, 2 oz chopped mushroom.

Remove the breasts from the birds, and portion. Sauté in hot butter, season lightly and set aside. Make a stock from the bird remainders and other ingredients except mushrooms, then thicken it with a flour and butter roux. Pass through a sieve, adjust seasoning, add chopped mushrooms and re-heat until tender. Place breasts on a serving dish and cover with the thick sauce.

PIGEON

ONE THING IS CERTAIN about woodpigeon - they are consistently good to eat. I've never wanted to try and prove or disprove the prediction that if you eat a pigeon a day for a week you'll be dead, but during the early post war years, pigeon often appeared on our menu twice or three times a week. I've never tasted a bad one, and I've had them cooked in all sorts of ways. While I would not rate them in any way superior to other 'game', they do have this quality of being consistent. The meat always tastes the same whether they've been feeding on corn or clover, rape or radish. Certain of the smaller doves can be less reliable, but the 'woody' remains constant, which is more than can be said for a lot of other hunted game.

It is customary for some shooters to pluck their shot birds while they wait in the hide for others to come. It makes sense to do so, and saves problems at home. It is not strictly necessary to pluck pigeon, however, and for purposes of stewing or pie making, there's a lot to be said for cutting out just the breasts. It's a simple operation. Just cut off the wings, break open the skin on the breast, put a finger behind the 'wishbone' and pull. There is, after all, very little meat left once the breast has been removed and the method is not particularly wasteful. I practice it a lot myself because I find the remainders very useful for the ferrets. None of my game is ever wasted.

The common woodpigeon or ring dove is not everyone's idea of good eating, but that is no excuse for shooting them and leaving them in heaps to rot as I have seen done many times - too late to do anything about it. It is not advisable to keep pigeon too long before either cooking or freezing. Dressed birds can be put into deep freeze on the same day; those to be cooked are better, perhaps, left until the next.

After cleaning, plucked birds should be washed thoroughly and cleaned inside and out. A soft, round-headed dish-washing brush is ideal for cleaning out the inside.

When all traces of blood have been removed, the birds can be left to drain and later dried off with a cloth. The practice of not washing out birds (as with fowl) does not apply to pigeon.

One of my favourite pigeon dishes using whole plucked birds is to stuff them with raw minced beef, a similar amount of plain boiled rice, a liberal helping of minced onion, salt, pepper and a hint of rosemary. After stuffing, place in a casserole dish, pour over a thick brown sauce made with a brown roux, stock, diced onions and carrots, cover the dish and bake in a moderate oven for $1\frac{1}{2}$ hours or until the meat is about to fall off the bones. If you like meat cooked in wine, add a glass of claret or port to the sauce. Some finely chopped mushrooms will enhance the dish which I like to serve with fondant potatoes and any vegetables in season.

Most early-season birds (that is to say, those taken in October) are likely to prove tender and suitable for roasting.

Make up a forcemeat stuffing from brown bread, fried onion, sage, suet, salt, pepper and the minced giblets from the birds. Stuff and pack into a deep baking dish, spreading any surplus forcemeat between the birds. Cover with layers of streaky pork and roast in a moderate oven. Remove the streaky pork and brown off the tops of the birds before serving.

Pigeon pie can be prepared in many more or less traditional ways. There is scope for imagination and there are no really hard and fast rules except that the cooked birds are portioned, covered with thick gravy and baked in a pie. A typical recipe would be as follows:

Stew together 2 pigeons (quartered), ½ lb diced stewing steak, ¼ lb diced ham, a sliced onion, a hint of mixed herbs, pepper and salt. When cooked, thicken the stock with brown roux or a commercial gravy thickener, place all in a large pie dish and cover with short crust or puff pastry. Brush with milk and/or beaten egg and bake off at 400°F until golden. Serve hot with potatoes and vegetables.

A variation on an old traditional recipe calls for the raw baking of 12 portions of pigeon (3 birds), 1 lb lean beef, ½ lb lean bacon, 3 hard-boiled eggs, and shortcrust pastry. Halve the eggs, slice the beef and bacon thinly and place all in a pie dish along with the pigeon portions. Season and half cover with stock. Cover with pastry crust and bake at about 425°F for 20 minutes with a covering of kitchen foil over the pastry. Remove from the oven, brush the pastry over with egg glaze and bake for another hour and a half at 325°F or thereabouts. When cooked, top up with stock poured in through the pastry vent.

This pie may be served hot or cold, but if intended as a cold dish, the remaining stock should be 'jellied' with gelatine or boiled with a pig's trotter so that it sets firmly when cold. This cold dish is improved by the addition of a pinch of sage in the final stage.

A fine tasting pâté may be made from well-cooked pigeon, pork, thyme, onions and seasoning. Traditionally, it is all minced and baked in a bacon-lined dish, but a simpler method is to pressure-cook it all (equal parts of pigeon and pork) in a minimum of stock, season, remove the bones and pass it through a fine mincer twice. This makes a rough pâté which may be improved in many ways, by additions to suit the cook's taste.

A little brandy, a spoonful of made-up English mustard, a wedge of butter, some finely minced bacon pieces or liver of any kind may be pounded into the pâté as it cools, singly or in any combination. A firmer pâté will result if the warm mix is left in its dish or basin overnight with a heavy weight. (A large saucepan of water provides sufficient weight). If you are keen an garlic, a little may be added in the cooking, or garlic salt may be used to season. Don't worry too much about weights or measures; use a little imagination and find out for yourself what is *good* and what is *better*. Nothing will ever be bad!

I refer to one of my own concoctions as 'pigeon peppers'. It's a simple dish that serves as a means of using up pigeon breasts when they are more than plentiful.

Mince together two parts pigeon breast and one part (roughly by weight if you're fussy) lean beef. Mix in some minced raw onion, plain boiled rice, tomato purée and mixed herbs. Season with salt and pepper. Remove the pulp from several green peppers and fill them with the meat and rice mixture. Place in a deep casserole dish, half cover with thickened stock, lay rashers of streaky bacon on top, cover dish and bake slowly at about 350°F until all is tender. Cook any remaining meat and rice mixture either separately or in with the peppers. This is a fairly rich and filling dish.

The fact that only the breast meat is used does not indicate wastage. The pigeon remainders, including legs, necks and giblets, serve to make the necessary stock or, if pressure-cooked with mixed vegetables, can be transformed into a soup.

If the rice in the foregoing 'recipe' is replaced by dried breadcrumbs and the meat mixture is bound by a raw egg, it can be moulded into croquette shapes and deep fried.

Strictly speaking, deep frying calls for some kind of coating such as egg and breadcrumbs, but if flat 'patty' shapes are moulded instead of the traditional cylindrical croquettes, they may be cooked in shallow fat very satisfactorily.

Young, early-season pigeon may also be grilled. Cut the birds in half and beat each half flat with a cleaver (or place them between two wooden chopping boards and hit with a clenched fist!), sprinkle with tenderiser and leave for an hour or two, brush lightly with cooking oil, season and grill until crisp and tender. Do *not* try this with ancient birds or you'll regret it. You can usually tell if a bird is tender or not by pushing a finger into its breast. A young bird punctures easily, and with little pressure.

It goes without saying, of course, that some of these recipes will apply to other game, and in the case of the 'pigeon peppers', vegetable marrow will serve as an alternative to the peppers.

SNIPE AND WOODCOCK

NEITHER OF THESE species of game bird can be regarded as extremely popular by today's standards. Snipe are common enough in certain marshy areas, but I believe that fewer people shoot them these days because of the price of shotgun ammunition. I may be wrong, of course, but it seems that many of my own shooting friends do not hunt snipe as they used to do.

Woodcock may well be prolific in some parts of the country but I have never seen them in large numbers anywhere. It is well known among shooting men that a 'right and left' at woodcock (i.e. two birds killed consecutively with the right and left barrels of a shotgun) is a near impossibility.

For that reason there is very little to say about either bird that could not apply to the other smaller birds already discussed.

Traditionally, however, both snipe and woodcock are dressed without being drawn. The thought of cooking birds with the guts still in seems quite revolting to me, but that apparently is how it should be. The birds are trussed for roasting, but the head is skinned and left on; the long beak is passed through the legs and body to serve as a skewer.

Once again recipes for both birds call for the traditional toast, gravy, bacon and so forth. Old recipe books suggest that 'one bird may be served to a gentleman but a lady may be satisfied with half'.

Whether or not he or she is supposed to eat the lot is not stated, and on the few occasions that I have had sufficient snipe, woodcock or a mixture of both, I have treated them as I would do other small game birds. I skin them and cook them in a simple 'home-cooking' style. I have already mentioned the only snipe and starling pudding I ever ate, but it will do no harm to state that both snipe and woodcock (or a mixture of both) really are delicious if cooked as a steak-and-kidney-pudding. And why not? The same applies to pies, casseroles, grills and a host of other dishes.

There is no need to stick strictly to one type of game bird or animal. They all mix well and there is no reason why a couple of snipe should not be padded out with a little beef, pork or veal to make a pleasant dish for several people. To waste those two snipe 'because there's not enough to go round' is the real sin. Both snipe and woodcock have tender skins and it is worth remembering that if they are to be plucked, special care is needed not to tear them. (Yet another reason for my decision to skin all, or nearly all, my game birds.)

Just for interest's sake, however, let me pass on a couple of recipes acquired in America recently. The old gentleman who gave them to me said that it was doubtful if one hunter in a hundred had ever seen snipe or woodcock but those that knew the birds would never miss the opportunity of eating them. He insisted that they should be plucked and dressed as quickly as possible after being shot.

Roast Snipe

Pick, clean and wash out four snipe, season them inside and out with salt and pepper, and wipe a piece of garlic over them. Toast four pieces of bread, cook the snipes very quickly in a skillet of hot butter, basting them as they cook. After 10 minutes, dust the birds with flour and brown them off, basting all the time.

Put the toast, well buttered, into a baking dish, lay a snipe on each piece and finish in a slow oven. Serve with slices of orange or orange jelly.

Well at least that one is different!

Roast Woodcock

Pick, clean and season the bird inside and out. Cover completely with thinly sliced fat bacon and cook in a hot oven until the bacon shrivels. Reduce heat to 350oF and add about 2 oz of butter and a $\frac{1}{4}$ pint of full cream. Cook until birds are tender and serve on toast with the sauce.

Woodcock Mexicana

Two woodcock, lemon juice, minced onion, lard, flour, saffron, minced green pepper.

Remove the meat from the bones, cut into small portions, place in a basin and squeeze a lemon over it. Season with salt and pepper, dredge with flour and fry in hot lard with the other ingredients, stirring continuously. Pour over a whole tin of tomato soup, cover and cook for 20 minutes.

WILDFOWL

'THE FEW WILD GEESE my husband brings home during the early season usually taste either of glue, cod liver oil or ointment' a housewife once told me. 'We enjoy rabbit and other game, so how about telling us how to cook knobbly-kneed wild geese?'

It's a long time since I shot a goose myself, but every year I end up with at least one for the pot from friends who are not only keener shots, but who seem to like crawling through mud at 5 a.m. on a winter's morning. I'm glad they do, I'm not averse to wild goose; though I have never had one tasting like glue or ointment. The occasional cod liver oil tasting specimen has come my way though, and I really don't know what's to be done about it.

I go to the Solway most years; no longer to shoot geese, but to join up with old friends, drink a little whisky, and tell a lot of lies. Every so often one of my keen wildfowler friends reports a fishy-flavoured bird too, so I'm sure it's not imagination on my part.

Since I've treated wild goose in exactly the same way as I've dealt with pheasant, however, I have not experienced a really unpleasant tasting bird. This means, of course, that my geese are skinned and not plucked; and, although it is a gory business, I believe strongly in skinning the birds before they have cooled if possible. I've no idea if this action could be proved to have any effect on the flavour of the meat, but it always appears to me to be the case.

One idea passed on to me by an American goose hunter is worth recording. It's simple enough and it's easy to see why it brings about such an improvement in the meat flavour. I don't think it matters whether the goose has been plucked or skinned, but it should be placed in cold salt water to which a little lemon juice or vinegar has been added.

Then it should be brought to the boil and removed from the heat at once. This helps remove some of the bloodshot spots and makes the meat mild flavoured and less strong tasting than usual.

After that, of course, it has to be cooked in any of the usual ways. And, just as with other kinds of game, there are scores of ways of preparing goose for the table.

I have a special liking for skinned and roasted goose with apples, onions and streaky pork.

Prepare the carcase by the quick-boiling method first, clean well inside and out and rub the inside with a mixture of salt and ground black pepper. Fill the inside with chopped onion and sliced apples (a little dried breadcrumb and sage, too, if you fancy it).

Place all in a roasting dish with about 6 oz butter, 2 rashers of streaky pork, and ¾ pint water. Stir in a little flour while the water is still cold, and cook all slowly until the water has reduced. Baste the bird with the butter and streaky pork drippings until crisp, and tender. Make a rich gravy from the roasting dish residue by adding a little more water, boiling furiously and removing most of the floating grease. Serve with a separate dish of apple sauce.

Wild goose is not everyone's choice of game. But many are shot each year and not eaten and I cannot find it in my heart to excuse such behaviour. There are many more ways of making wild goose presentable and the old excuse that the product is either too tough, too strong, or too dry, is sheer eyewash.

Try serving an apple sauce made up with apples, brown sugar, butter, lemon juice and white wine. Don't be too fussy about the quantities - just add and taste until it's about right. Boil the whole lot together to form a purée. Add a clove or two if you think fit. Put in the tiniest hint of cochineal if you like a rose-coloured sauce. This does nothing to improve the taste at all, but it does add attraction to the dish.

I've mentioned before that I always believe in washing out my game thoroughly before cooking. Why anyone should not want to amuses and amazes me. A clean cloth will dry both the inside and outside of a wild goose after it has been washed and drained. To make sure of mine, I squirt it out under pressure by putting my finger over the end of the tap.

Any badly shot goose *needs* this kind of treatment and it's a good idea after it has dried out thoroughly to sprinkle the inside with a little vinegar and leave a large raw onion inside overnight. The following day, remove the onion, dredge the bird liberally with seasoned flour (if it is a particularly lean bird, spread it lightly with pure lard first).

If you want to use one of the regular forcemeat stuffings, there is no reason for not doing so, but wild goose roasted without any kind of dressing is fine. *Do* be careful about those tough old leader birds, however. They're usually recognisable and they should not be roasted. Put them in a casserole or jug as you would a hare and cook them for as long as you like, but not less than $2\frac{1}{2}$-3 hours.

Don't be afraid to mince goose meat (it minces better if it is boiled quickly as already described) and use it for various kinds of pâtés, croquettes, olives, or pies.

Obviously different people have different ideas of what tastes good and what doesn't, but let me tell you about one of my favourite goose concoctions.

Slice all the breast meat thinly and keep the slices as large as possible. A thick, stubby portion can be slit halfway through and flattened, two small slices can be pounded together to make one piece if necessary. These slices are to become wrapping pieces for the following mixture.

Pressure cook the goose remainders along with one ham shank, an onion and *very little* stock. Remove all the meat and fat from the bones, and pass all through a fine mincer. Season to taste (watch the salt because of that contained in the ham shank), add a little sage, and dry off if necessary with a little breadcrumb.

Form the mixture into sausage or croquette shapes and wrap them into the goose slices to make small, sealed parcels. (A variation on the old beef olive theme). Thicken and season the remaining stock to make a savoury gravy. Pack the parcels into a baking dish. Cover with gravy, put a lid or foil cover over the baking dish, and cook at about 350°F for 1½ hours or until all is tender.

I wouldn't insult regular wild fowlers or their wives who obviously know how to deal with their game, but to those who have had bad experiences with greylags and pinks, I offer these suggestions.

It's nice to go home after two or three days and wave a brace of birds in front of those who doubt your hunting ability, but it's better, from the culinary point of view, to dress the birds out quickly, put them in plastic bags and get them chilled or frozen as soon as possible after they are shot.

Looked after properly at the beginning, wild goose is superb food, and I reckon this is borne out by the immortal words of a dear old friend of mine who died a few years ago.

'A wild goose is a stupid bird,' he said. 'Jest too much for a meal for one, but not enough for two.'

There is little to add about the preparation of other wild fowl. Some like to pluck their teal, mallard, wigeon and other species of duck and, perhaps, if the object is to roast them to perfection, plucking gives that extra crispness which is found in thick, fatty skin of wild duck.

There are as many ways of cooking duck as any other kind of game, of course, but when the bird is to be roasted purely and simply with or without stuffing, with or without traditional orange salad or orange sauce, let me offer a word or two of advice. Quick boiling in advance, as with geese, will take away any hint of fishy flavour. In truth very few wild duck ever taste fishy, but some *do*. They are, in my opinion, inedible, but if subjected to the quick boiling treatment, with a good measure of salt added to the water, that problem is usually eliminated. It may not be necessary but it is surely better to be safe than sorry.

Most recipes for wild duck of any kind suggest that the bird should be roasted and served slightly underdone to preserve the flavour. Tastes differ, of course, but I have yet to sample an undercooked duck that tasted better than one that was slightly overcooked (and I have a host of friends who agree with me).

One of our local inns specialises in roast duck and it has always been recognised as the 'house speciality', highly recommended by all who have tried it. We were interested enough to learn the secret and asked the chef how he managed to serve excellent roast duck so consistently. He told us that it was because he cooked them for longer than usual. 'My ducks are cooked through completely,' he stated. 'The outside is crisp, the inside slightly overcooked. That is how roast duck should be served.'

My own roasting method is as follows. After trussing (and stuffing if desired), spread the whole of the bird with a covering of pure lard, then dust liberally with seasoned flour before putting in a roasting dish. Cook in a hot oven for about 8 minutes, then lower heat and baste frequently until tender. Time taken can be anything from 30 minutes to an hour depending upon the size and quality of the bird.

The residue left in the baking dish can be transformed into good gravy by adding a little stock or water and skimming off the floating grease. If you like that kind of thing you can add a little port wine to the gravy before serving. An orange and lettuce salad comprised of broken (not cut) lettuce and finely sliced orange rings with peel and pips removed can be served separately. A little salad oil or (if preferred) a little brandy will enhance this particular salad.

A simple, traditional orange sauce can also be served with wild duck and while there are many recipes available, a good quality end product can be produced by boiling the thinly sliced peel of two oranges in about ¾ pint of clear stock. When tender add the juice of the oranges plus a little lemon juice and, if available, a tablespoonful of redcurrant jelly. Thicken the sauce with a white roux (but don't *over-thicken*), season and serve.

Duck that have been skinned either for convenience's sake, or to provide one more variation on the roast duck theme, are better covered with pork slices before roasting. The natural skin covering is then to some extent replaced and the birds will not go dry.

The same trimmings may be served with it, but a rich brown sauce made by adding flour to the natural drippings and browning off before adding water or stock is perhaps more desirable than traditional orange sauce.

Skinned birds can also be portioned and cooked slowly in white sauce with the addition of a little lemon juice, a bay leaf, a finely chopped onion and a pinch of thyme. Seasoned with black pepper and salt and served with croutons or tiny squares of freshly baked pastry, this makes an excellent main course and is a good way of using up left-overs. It goes without saying that button mushrooms will further improve this dish and if the whole dish is browned quickly under a grill before serving it will appear even more appetising.

If all bones are removed from this left-over, fricassee-type dish it can be covered with puff pastry and served in pie form. If the meat is chopped finely and the sauce made slightly thicker than usual, the mixture may be added to vol-au-vent cases and served either as a main course or snack meal depending upon the quantity available.

Most duck recipes involving cooking with wine call for claret or burgundy, presumably because the meat is dark, but friends who have experimented with dry white wines and cider say that they prefer these to the traditional additives. I have no feelings one way or the other. I will use wines to cook for other folk; but as explained before, wine does nothing to improve the taste of any food for me.

SOME WILD FOWL RECIPES

Fine Casserole

Remove bones from any wildfowl and chop the meat finely. Add diced onions, carrots, chopped mushrooms, herbs and spices to taste, and an equal amount of chopped ham, bacon or beef. Cover all with a brown sauce made from the pressure-cooked remaining bones and a brown roux. Cook slowly in a moderate oven until the sauce is thick and the meat tender.

Whole Casserole

Cut duck or goose into serving portions and fry briskly in hot shallow fat. Remove from pan and add chopped carrots, onions, mushrooms, celery stalks and a little shredded white cabbage. Toss vegetables in pan until they begin to brown, dust liberally with flour, salt, pepper, and mixed herbs. Cover with good stock, add wildfowl portions, bring to boil, transfer to a casserole dish and cook slowly with the lid on for about 1½ hours or until tender. This dish is improved or at least altered in taste by the addition of thinly cut orange peel strips. Freshly cooked green peas with plenty of mint flavouring and a pinch of sugar can be added to the sauce immediately before serving.

Braised Duck

Stuff the duck with sage, onions, the minced liver, heart and gizzard, a little finely chopped bacon and breadcrumbs. Cooked chestnuts may also be used if liked. Brown off on all sides and place in a roasting dish on a bed of thickly sliced and browned onions. (Thick onion slices can be browned directly on top of the fire plate of a solid fuel cooker - cleaned and lightly greased in advance of course - otherwise they are better browned in a preheated heavy iron frying pan.)

Pour thick brown sauce over duck and leave the breast exposed. Cook slowly in a low oven and turn bird if necessary to avoid drying out. The roasting dish can be covered with a lid or kitchen foil for the first ¾ hour or so but the whole dish should be browned nicely before removing from the oven.

Duck and Rice

Roast a fat mallard or teal in the usual style - cook it well and remove from the roasting dish. Strain off all the fat and make a rich gravy from what remains. Meanwhile cook a cupful of dark grain rice until tender and fluffy. Cool quickly under a cold tap and leave to drain. Re-heat the duck dripping in a heavy iron pan and toss in the cooked rice and one small finely chopped onion. Stir or shake continually and season while cooking with red pepper and salt.

Place the roasted duck in the centre of a hot serving dish and garnish with watercress, button mushrooms and orange slices before serving.

ROOKS

ROOKS COULD HARDLY be regarded as 'game' in the truest sense of the word but in this book I use the word in its widest sense and let it embrace rabbits, pigeon, rooks, wild fowl and all other kinds of edible wild-life. I can think of very little game I have not tried at one time or other. I have always, for instance, whenever possible, observed the May 13th rook shooting ritual, and I never cease to be amazed at the accuracy of it. Irrespective of the conditions that have prevailed during the past winter and spring, the peak rook-shooting period seldom varies by much more than 24 hours. In order to enjoy it at its best, it is necessary to watch the conditions carefully. Suddenly it's all over and (to coin an apt phrase) the birds have flown. There will be no more rook pie until next year.

Rook pie. When you look at a young squab and compare it with, say, a pigeon or a partridge, it doesn't appear very attractive. But take half a dozen breasts and bake them in a pie with hard boiled eggs and some ham shank or streaky bacon, and you have a feast to be remembered.

The season is short. Very short. Only the young birds are fit to eat and even then only the breasts and legs are used. The backs are bitter and quite inedible, so much so that some trainers will not allow their dogs to retrieve shot rooks.

The breast meat is exceptionally tender, however. It is white, and has a delicate taste. There are many ways of cooking it, the best known of which is the above-mentioned rook pie. But rook pie can take so many shapes and forms that it is hard to decide what is or is not traditional. I do not hesitate to recommend what I have always regarded as traditional, however, and while I do not pretend to know what actual chemical change (if any) takes place, let me outline the way one kind of rook pie has been prepared in my family for several generations.

After washing thoroughly, soak the breasts and legs of, say, half a dozen rooks in fresh milk overnight. Remove them from the dish and allow to drain off completely.

Line a round cake tin with short crust pastry and place inside it the rook meat (trimmed and boneless) with about an equal portion of chopped ham or bacon, and several hard-boiled eggs cut in halves. Part cover it all with clear, seasoned stock, put on a pastry lid, seal round the edges, and bake in a hot oven (425°F) for about 20 minutes. Glaze the top of the pie with beaten egg and continue cooking at 350°F for about another hour. Watch to see that the pastry lid does not over-bake. If it shows signs of doing so cover with a fold of brown paper or kitchen foil.

When cooked, fill up the pie (through the steam vent) with more stock (jellied) and serve cold with early spring salad.

What the soaking in milk does to the rooks is anyone's guess. I only know that it appears to improve the flavour and texture of the meat.

As it is almost white in colour, rook breast flesh really should not be cooked with a dark gravy; but who's being fussy? And why not mix it with some dark meat anyway? Some of the old 'country cottage recipes' for rook pie called for a pound of stewing beef, which had to be cooked well in advance because young rooks only take a few minutes or so to cook. Bearing this small fact in mind, there is no reason for not turning rooks into hot pies or casseroles with thick gravy. After trimming a dozen or so rooks (and leaving the breast and leg bones only for stock) there is very little actual meat to be cooked, but if it is diced (as nearly as it is possible to dice such a commodity), fried off in hot shallow fat with onions and carrots, dusted with flour, browned off and placed in a casserole dish to cook slowly with some good rich beef and gravy, the result is a meal with a distinctive and very wholesome flavour. If it is covered with a puff pastry lid it becomes a delicious hot pie.

If a covering of sliced raw potatoes is arranged on top and the dish is cooked 'hot-pot' style there is no game more tasty. And so it could go on; this is simple home cooking and applies to so many other different types of game and meat.

But let me tell of a different kind of dish. One that is quick to prepare, and, if you like, with a slightly more 'modern' flavour.

Fry together about half a pound of streaky bacon cut into small ($\frac{1}{4}$ in.) dice and a finely-chopped, biggish onion. Drain off the bacon from the fat. Into the fat, which has been brought up to 'smoke' heat again, toss as much (or as little) rook meat as you have available. This too should be cut into $\frac{1}{4}$ in. dice. Keep the meat well shaken or stirred until all is crisp and golden.

Meanwhile boil in salted water some long grain rice, and when it is barely cooked, run it under a cold tap to keep the grains separate. Drain it off thoroughly and toss it all into the remaining fat after the meat has been removed. Keep the pan very hot, stir or shake the rice until it has thoroughly re-heated, then add the bacon, onions and rook meat. Season at this stage but, because of the salt contained in the bacon, be cautious. Do not hesitate, however, to add whatever kind of other seasoning takes your fancy. My own preference is for cayenne pepper, but I'll go along with a little tabasco or Worcestershire sauce. Once again I have to emphasise that it is up to you to taste and adjust to your liking.

Most rook dishes are improved by the addition of some other kind of meat. Rook breasts alone, though by no means tasteless, do not have a strong flavour, and if you prefer to regard the meat as 'white' and cook it accordingly, there's justification in combining it with chicken. To be absolutely frank, I find the so-called 'broiler' chickens available today tasteless, and when mixing chicken with other game, I prefer to use portions of honest-to-goodness boiling fowl. These do have some flavour that reminds me of chicken, and is in no way reminiscent of cardboard or plastic. But, of course, it takes a little longer to cook.

It may be used in place of the beef, ham or bacon in the dishes already mentioned and any thick sauce needed for their completion can be of the white bechamel type.

There are, today, a number of canned 'cook-in' sauces available and there is no reason why they should not be used to present rook breast and leg portions in a somewhat different style. But there is no need to purchase these ready-made sauces if you've a mind to make your own. And the fun you can get out of making your own is the *different* tastes you can achieve.

It really doesn't matter a scrap whether you stick to recipes or not. The basis of many of my cook-in sauces is tomato juice. It comes most conveniently in a tin, but it can be made from stewed, soft tomatoes, tomato purée - even tomato soup at a push. I could not begin to tell you all the different ingredients you can put in if you wish, but just for interest's sake try some of the following: wine vinegar, cider vinegar, brown sugar, tabasco sauce, french mustard, garlic, finely chopped chives, salt (of course), dry white wine, and anything else obviously applicable that happens to appeal to you. If the sauce looks too thin, thicken it up with a white roux, or a little cornflour. Do not mix milky products with vinegar. It won't ruin the sauce, but it may curdle it and make it *appear* unpalatable.

Experiment, taste and then more experiment, will produce sauces much more exciting than those made to a strict formula, and if a large portion is made up, it can be stored in small cartons in the deep freeze for future use. Meanwhile it will undoubtedly add a little spice to the annual rook feast.

SALMON AND SEA TROUT

SALMON AND SEA TROUT are not the same fish but as their behaviour, habitat and flavour are virtually identical, it is fair to say that cooking methods can be the same for both species. The only qualification, perhaps, is that whereas mature salmon are always big (that is to say weighing at least 4 or 5 lb and up to as much as 30 or 40 lb), sea trout do not reach such proportions and many are caught weighing less than 1 lb.

Both species are migratory and go to sea after about 18 months in the river of their birth. They return to the same river to spawn and their size depends more or less upon how long they have been at sea.

A salmon that returns to spawn after two years is referred to as a grilse. A sea trout that returns within a year (having perhaps ventured only to the estuary) is immature and is referred to by a number of local names, the most common of which is herling.

These are takeable fish, and their subtle flavour defies description. They are my own personal favourite, and I am sure (arctic char excepted) they are the world's most delicious fish.

One sees fish referred to as salmon trout in fish markets and, despite the Trades Description Act, some of these are rainbow trout. This is totally inaccurate for there can be no possible connection. There is no such fish as a salmon trout. The brown trout (*Salmo Trutta*) and the sea trout which is simply a migratory brown trout might answer to the description in a court of law, but there is no excuse for referring to rainbow trout as salmon trout.

I mention this only in passing. I hope this book will be read by the wives of anglers who know how to catch fish, but it is possible for the average housewife to become confused regarding the pet names traditionally given to weird fish by perfectly honest fishmongers, who presumably accept the names given by the wholesalers.

I not pretend to understand it. I have seen dogfish of one kind or another marked up as 'rock salmon', 'hake' and 'conger', and I could quote many more examples.

Fresh-run salmon and sea trout, that is to say fish that have only just left the sea, are of top quality, and are expensive. They are full of natural oil, their flesh is red and they have a silver sheen about their skin which tells its own story. Sea lice still clinging to the fish indicate that it is fresh from the sea.

After moving upstream for several weeks, or even months, the silver sheen disappears, the skin darkens, the flesh pales, and there comes a time, just before spawning, when it is hardly worth eating. After spawning, of course, the fish is inedible and it is illegal to retain it if caught.

Little remains now but to describe the various methods of cooking salmon, sea trout and herling; and because very few anglers are likely to have a surplus of salmon, I will confine my remarks to traditional recipes which I know to be safe. No-one would care to experiment with the season's only salmon, I'm sure.

I will add one more item of interest, however. It is customary for anglers, who catch an old, dark or 'stale' salmon, to send it off to be smoked. These old fish are often referred to as 'smokers', but it is a mistake. No amount of smoking will turn a poor fish into a good one. If you want to send a fish to be smoked by the professionals, send them one which they themselves can envy. Only a rich, oily, fresh-run salmon will make a prime smoker. Old or 'stale' fish will be returned in a perfectly edible condition, but smoking will not improve them.

Steamed Salmon (whole)

Gut and gill the fish, taking care to clean along the inside of the backbone thoroughly. This can be done by picking out the dark portions with a pointed knife and scrubbing lightly with the tufted end of a regular scrubbing brush.

Smaller fish can be cleaned with a nail brush or tooth brush. Sprinkle the fish liberally with salt and cook it over boiling water so that the fish is completely enveloped by steam. Obviously a large 'kettle' with a suitable grille is needed for this kind of cooking, which is practised more in large establishments than in the home. Nevertheless for special parties this style of cooking retains the flavour and allows the whole fish to be skinned and presented attractively. At some stage of the cooking it may have to be turned, but if the kettle lid fits correctly it should not be necessary.

Now for the artistry.

When the fish is cooked and before it has completely cooled, remove skin from the upper side and as much from the back (including the fins which should pull clear) as possible. Now place a large, oval serving plate over the grille holding the fish. Grip both plate and grille firmly and turn everything over so that the plate is now underneath and the grille uppermost. Remove the skin from the lower side (which is now uppermost) and mop up any surplus juice on the serving plate with a paper kitchen towel. Remove the eyes from the fish and replace them with stuffed olives.

Peel a cucumber and scratch it all round lengthwise with a kitchen fork. Cut it into thin slices (which will now have taken on a serrated appearance). Cut up several lemons into thin slices. Slice up some tinned button mushrooms. Thaw and dry off some frozen prawns. Chop up some hard-boiled eggs very finely.

Boil up some plain, white rice in salt water, and when fluffy refresh under a cold tap and drain. Prepare some lettuce leaves and watercress and let your imagination run riot. Surround the fish with the rice and decorate it all with the other ingredients. The scope for presentation of this dish is never-ending, and it is of little use my describing *any particular* method of decoration. It so happens that I choose to alternate lemon and cucumber slices overlapping along the centre of the fish, to add the prawns, mushrooms and chopped egg to the rice surround, and to overlap the plate edge with lettuce and watercress dressed up with the remaining lemon and cucumber. Very occasionally I add a little more colour with firm, sliced tomatoes and/or tender sweet corn.

Melted butter and lemon juice poured over the fish when it has cooled adds to the flavour. The whole dish, at party time, draws ooh's and ah's from all our guests and yet, in truth, there are no problems whatsoever involved in its preparation.

It *is* possible to serve the same dish hot, but this is a little more difficult because the final decoration has to be done at speed. However, if the plate is crackling hot to begin with and all the ingredients (except those obviously used cold) are kept on a hot plate, it *can* be done. What is more, the dish can then be served with any or several of the sauces recommended earlier for fish.

I usually serve three, cheese, prawn, and egg and I find that most of our guests sample all of them. But here's the good part. Any left-overs can be put together and made into yet another hot dish which I can only think of as kedgeree.

Salmon Kedgeree
Flake cold salmon off the bones and mix into a casserole dish with left-over rice, prawns, mushrooms and chopped eggs. Mix together any left-over sauces and pour over the fish. Sprinkle with cayenne pepper, completely cover with grated cheese and bake in

a hot oven until bubbling. Place under a grill to brown off the top cheese layer and serve.

Salmon Cutlets

Wrap lightly buttered cutlets in foil after sprinkling with salt, pepper, lemon juice and/or a little vinegar. Cook either in a hot oven or over a pan of boiling water on the stove top. This recipe will, of course, serve for any kind of fish portion, cutlet or fillet.

Whole sea trout can be cooked in exactly the same way.

Grilled Sea Trout

Fillet and remove the skin from sea trout weighing up to about 3 lb and cut up into sizeable portions. Sprinkle with salt, pepper and lemon juice, spread with butter or soft margarine and cook *quickly* under a *hot* grill. Many cooks spoil the delicate flavour of grilled sea trout by cooking too slowly for too long. Cooked quickly the fish remains moist and retains its flavour. Do not heat up the grill while the fish is below it; heat it up well in advance.

Breakfast Herling

(I cannot close this chapter without mention of my favourite breakfast.) Clean and head as many small herling as you can eat. Roll them in seasoned flour and place in a baking dish. Cover with prime back bacon rashers and cook in a hot oven or under a grill. Remove the bacon when it is cooked and brown off the herling on both sides. Serve with hot toast; and if you caught the herling during the night (as is always the case with me) retire to bed at once.

Herling and bacon go together beautifully and the alternative to the above recipe is to cook them together in the same heavy frying pan.

There are many other ways of preparing them, of course, and there is no reason for them all to be retained for breakfast, but while there are many other fish to be caught and cooked, none fits the breakfast bill of fare like the gleaming silver herling.

So we will save some of the other recipes for less attractive fish and leave it there.

TROUT

THERE ARE THREE species of trout and several hybrid trouts in the British Isles today. Only the brown trout is native. Rainbow trout were introduced over a hundred years ago, and American brook trout much later. Since then, hybrids have been produced between brown trout and rainbow trout and have been given the names 'brownbow' and 'sunbeam' (depending on parental sex). Little has been heard of them since.

Hybrid rainbow X brook trout have been produced more recently and, again, depending upon parental sex, are known by the names 'tiger trout' and 'cheetah trout'. These hybrids appear to be almost certainly sterile, but time alone will tell the full story.

Today the rainbow trout has learned to spawn and reproduce in a very few special waters, but the vast majority are raised by trout farmers for stocking reservoirs and enclosed waters all over the country. Trout fishing, particularly rainbow trout fishing, is booming and at last many of the old die-hards are accepting the fact that fish caught from fresh water can be good to eat.

Native brown trout differ so much from water to water that they could almost be regarded as different species. Yet the tiny troutlet from the Scottish burn, the Welsh hill stream or the Cumbrian beck is identical (apart from size) to the monstrous trout of the Irish and Scottish lochs, and the fertile chalk streams of the south. Their diet has an undoubted effect upon their flavour and there are a few waters that produce trout of poor quality. In the main, however, most stocked waters produce good, fat, pink-fleshed trout and it matters little to the cook whether they are browns or rainbows. A trout is a trout is a trout; and there's an end to it.

It is important, as I have already explained, to keep trout fresh after they are caught.

The American method of 'stringing' them alive to swim tethered until departure time, is really the most sensible solution to the whole problem; but so emotional are the British that they would rather kill their trout and watch them deteriorate through the day. Strung and left in the cold chalkstreams where I fish, freshly killed rainbow trout keep perfectly until I am ready to leave. Then I gut and gill them, place them in an insulated cooler box containing a plastic ice bottle. After a hundred-mile journey they are ice-cold, firm and ready for the freezer.

A simple cooler box can be made by lining a plywood, hardboard, or even a stout cardboard box with sheets of 1 in. thick polystyrene. The bottom and lid should be covered too, of course. A couple of old washing-up liquid bottles will serve as ice containers if nothing else is available, but those one-gallon screw-top containers are better. These provide cold water for drinks during a hot day as well as protection for freshly-caught fish. Never screw the caps on the bottles while they are freezing. Never try to use glass bottles. And never fill any container more than three-quarters full, to allow for the ice expansion.

If it appears that I have over-emphasised this need for keeping trout fresh, let me remind you that many are caught during the height of summer. Unlike perch and pike, which are autumn and winter fish (generally speaking), and sea trout which are often caught in the cool of the night, trout can quickly become flyblown and sun dried.

Get your trout home in good condition and they will serve to swell the contents of your freezer and impress your guests. Fail to do so and you might as well dig a hole and bury them.

As with all kinds of fish, there are many ways of cooking trout and I can only recommend that you try some of the recipes that follow. All have been tried, tested and enjoyed. It would be difficult to choose between them. It also goes without saying that any of the salmon and sea trout recipes already mentioned apply equally to brown and rainbow trout.

SOME TROUT RECIPES

Pan fried Troutlets
Tiny trout from the hill streams are delicious if cooked quickly and immediately after catching. Head and clean the fish and roll them in seasoned flour. Melt fresh butter or bacon fat in a thick frying pan until smoking. Place in the trout and tip in about ½ lb of almonds. Keep stirring the almonds while the underside of the troutlets turn crisp. Then turn over each fish carefully and continue cooking until the almonds are brown and the fish crisp on both sides. Allow to drain off on a kitchen towel before serving.

Boiled Trout (medium sized rainbow)
Clean and head the trout (or leave the head on if you prefer to be traditional, but remove the gills), place in a fish kettle and barely cover with salted water to which has been added a bay leaf. Replace the lid and simmer *very* slowly for 15 minutes or until the flesh is tender. Remove from water, drain, remove skin and spread liberally inside and out with butter. Squeeze with lemon juice and serve with any suitable white sauce.

Trout and Cheese Grill
Fillet the trout, spread with butter, and place under a grill for 5 minutes. Remove, turn the fillet over and smother with mature

cheddar cheese. Season with salt and a little cayenne pepper and continue grilling until the cheese is brown and the fish tender.

Baked Trout (An American recipe)

One 3 lb trout, 2 egg yolks, $\frac{1}{2}$ cup of finely chopped onion, $\frac{1}{4}$ lb butter, chopped parsley, chopped capers, sweet pickles, lemon juice, vinegar, salt and paprika.

Fillet the trout, remove the skin and then place the two halves together. Bake in a well-buttered dish for 15 minutes, then mix together the other ingredients and spread over the fish. Continue baking until cooked through.

Trout in White Wine Sauce (an American recipe)

Place trout fillets in a casserole dish and cover with a regular white sauce, to which has been added $\frac{1}{4}$ pint of white wine, 1 finely chopped onion, 2 well-beaten egg yolks, a tablespoonful of cream, a squeeze of lemon juice and some finely chopped parsley. Cover the dish and cook slowly in a cool oven. If the sauce separates, remove the fish and whisk with an egg beater before serving.

Trout in Tomato Sauce

Lay fillets in a casserole dish and cover with thickened, tinned tomato juice. (Use a white roux to thicken). Stir in a little tomato ketchup and cook until tender. Do *not* overcook.

Fried trout fillets

Cut fillets into fingers and make them completely dry. Dip in beaten egg and roll in powdered instant potato. Fry in oil until crisp.

Obviously the *powdered* instant potato is just another variation on the egg-and-breadcrumb theme, but it is novel and leads to other thoughts in the cooking of trout. Breadcrumbs and/or powdered potato can be replaced by ground-up crackers, savoury biscuits, and packet snacks. There are scores of them to choose from and they will all powder up finely if passed through a mincer or churned up in an ordinary liquidiser or blender.

PIKE

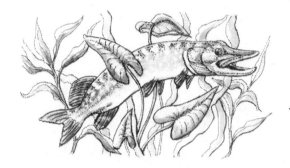

MENTION COOKING a pike and it's a racing certainty that someone will say 'Ah, quenelles de brochet'. Heaven knows why. Some may like them, and while I respect their taste, I do not share it. There are heartier ways of producing what are little more than fish cakes with a fancy name.

What about the good old English way with fluffy mashed potatoes and snow-white fish flakes mixed about half and half? Difficult to shape and cook because they tend to break up? Add a couple of knobs of lard to the mix - not butter or margarine or white fat, but *lard*. About as much as you'd add butter to a pan of mashed potatoes. Lacking in flavour? Add a squirt of anchovy essence, or a finely chopped onion, a generous sprig of chopped parsley, a pinch of sage, a hint of rosemary, a little paprika, half a tin of pilchards or whatever else you like. Let your hair down; be different.

However, do not dream up concoctions that completely disguise the flavour of the main ingredient. I once gave one of Izaak Walton's carp recipes to Ted Trueblood of Nampa, USA. He

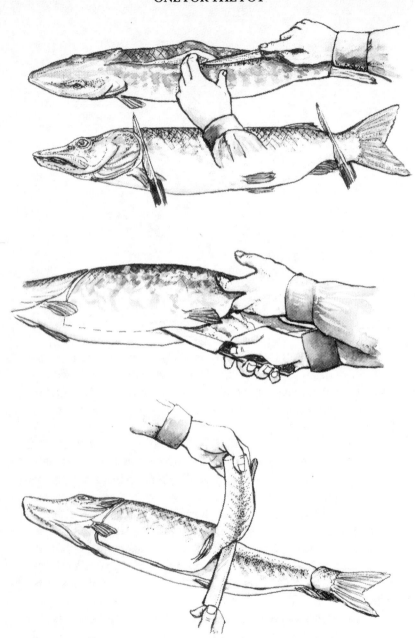

Three stages in filleting a pike

reckoned that even an old sock would taste good if so cooked but it was not a carp dish. I took his point.

Cook fish, fish cakes or fillets in oil by all means, but if you want a change try frying them in bacon fat. Pike are particularly good like that.

Try pike fillets, smeared with butter and a little barbecue sauce, *double* wrapped in foil and cooked over coals or barbecue bricks.

The method of filleting pike is illustrated here but if the thought of filleting scares you, take a sharp, heavy-duty knife, and after gutting the pike, slice it up into cutlets. These are cooked 'on the bone' like cod fillets, of course, and according to some accounts they are better that way. I have enough problems with bones, even in filleted portions, and I prefer not to make cutlets. Pike have lots of small, forked bones in their flesh and these have to be removed in the eating.

They are not likely to be missed and the chances of a 'bone in the throat' are highly unlikely. The important thing is to remember they are there.

Some traditional recipes suggest that pike should be left whole, but unless a mini-banquet is anticipated, what do you do with the left-overs from a 12 or 14-pounder? Pike of this size are not rare, and when they are removed from chalk streams (where they are undesirable) they are usually killed. Those who appreciate pike to eat take them away to be cooked. Those who are highly emotional about killing fish try to transport them to other waters where they are welcomed as extra stock. Those who don't like pike in any way, shape or form simply chuck them up the bank to rot. These are the wasteful anglers who need to be shown that pike *are* good to eat.

Large pike are regarded as sport fish by most coarse fishermen and I would not remove one unless it was badly hooked or so large as to warrant the attentions of a taxidermist. I will only take away large pike from waters where it is my duty to do so. Then I take them away for food and if they are too large to cook whole I have to fillet and portion them. Other anglers would be wise, in these days of highly expensive sea fish, to do the same.

Pike fillets can be cooked in any way applicable to other fish with large firm flakes. They are, in my opinion, better than cod when fried in batter in the traditional English fish 'n' chips style. The flesh is firmer and needs slightly longer cooking but otherwise there is no difference. It is perhaps worth mentioning in passing that a flour batter made with milk, and/or eggs, though much richer than the traditional batter made with water, browns off much too quickly for chunky fish like pike. The batter becomes dark long before the fish has cooked, and nothing tastes much worse than half-raw pike flesh. Make the batter with flour, salt, water and a pinch of baking powder; that's all.

Let the pike fillets or portions drain well, dry them off with a cloth, dip into the fairly thick batter and then at once into deep smoking fat or oil.

A non-stick frying pan will take care of unfloured or plain raw fish if no coating is required. Fried in an absolute minimum of fat or oil, pike retains its flavour and (for the weight-conscious) it does not contain as many calories as when floured or battered.

Pike are better when cooked as quickly after catching as possible. If they come from clean water they do *not* need the traditional soaking in salt water (who dreamed that one up I've no idea); if they come from foul water, no amount of soaking or salting will improve them.

It has been my pleasure and delight many times to catch a pike, take it ashore and have it in the pan within minutes of landing it. *That* is the finest way of eating pike, or indeed any other kind of fish. I do not know of any fresh water fish that improves with keeping.

Occasionally I catch a five or six pounder from the trout stream by accident on my fly rod, and I welcome it rather than curse it. I have access to lots of trout fishing, but because of the emotional attitudes prevalent among coarse fish anglers, all too few pike for the table come my way. I reserve the right to take away one or two each season from waters where the licence allows their removal, and in the event that I choose to take a fish in the four to five pound category it may very well end up cooked whole according to one or other of the traditional recipes. In America, northern pike are regarded as prime game fish; over here we tend to regard them as inedible vermin.

SOME PIKE RECIPES

Baked Pike fingers

Cut fillets into fingers and dip into milk. Cover with fine breadcrumbs, sprinkle liberally with pepper and salt and place in a well oiled baking dish. Put a knob of butter onto each finger and bake in a very hot oven (500°F) for about 15 minutes.

Baked Whole Pike

Remove the head (it looks terrible) and guts. Scale and cut out the fins with a fillet knife. Sprinkle the inside with salt and pepper after having removed the dark blood portion along the backbone. Stuff with any desired dressing or forcemeat and sew up the stomach cavity.

Score the fish deeply on both sides, place in a well-oiled dish, spread with butter and bake in a very hot oven (500°F) basting often with the natural juices until browned.

Stuffed fillets of Pike

Cut fillets into thin strips with a sharp knife. Spread each portion with a savoury stuffing and roll up into cylinder shapes. Lay in a greased baking dish with halved tomatoes separating. Sprinkle with cayenne pepper, cover with thin bacon rashers and bake in a hot (450°F) oven until it is crisp and tender.

Fried Pike fingers

Cut fillets into fingers, dry off with a cloth, sprinkle with salt and pepper, dip in beaten egg and then into bread or savoury biscuit crumbs. Fry in hot, deep fat.

Poached Fillets

Leave pike fillets large, lay in a buttered baking dish, sprinkle with salt and cayenne pepper. Half cover with milk, dot with butter,

and simmer slowly with the dish covered. Add a little white wine
if desired and use the natural juices to make or add to a suitably
flavoured white sauce.

Grilled Pike
   Fillet a small pike and leave the fillets whole. Dip each piece
in vegetable oil and allow to drain completely. Sprinkle with salt
and pepper and dredge lightly with flour. Dot with butter and cook
quickly under a hot grill.

PERCH

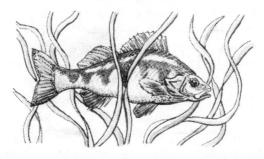

SINCE SOME WEIRD DISEASE, which spread like wildfire across England some years ago killing off perch by the countless thousands, there is, perhaps, an excuse for *not* taking large perch for the table, except from waters where they are an embarrassment. It was my practice, in the days when a number of our trout reservoirs held an abundance of perch, to buy a trout ticket and fish exclusively for perch. When I fished for trout and caught a perch accidentally, I welcomed it as another 'white' fish for the table. Perch, you see, despite what else may be said about them, are the finest, firmest and sweetest of all our coarse fish. When caught from clear streams and fly-only reservoirs, the flesh is clean-tasting and there is no hint of mud.

When I was able to catch several two-pounders at a sitting from the upper reaches of the Great Ouse, I always made a point of taking a couple twice a year for the table. I took them to reserve my right to do so *and* because I enjoyed cooking and eating them. I have eaten far more trout than perch and today I would willingly swap a two pound trout for a perch of the same size. I can catch a two pound trout any time I wish during the season; I would not know where to look for a two pound perch any more.

There are signs that they have made a tremendous comeback in many waters, however, and already 6-8 oz perch are proving troublesome. Perhaps these will grow to become pounders and eventually two pounders, but I fear that once they become firmly established the coarse fish angler's emotional policy of *never* killing fish will bring about more overcrowding. Countless thousands of small perch will be spawned, attain a weight of a couple of ounces and then grow no more. Perch are prolific breeders, and each water can only support a given poundage of fish. It would be better if some of those 6-8 ounce fish were removed and eaten. Then perhaps there would be a chance for some of the remainder to grow on to two pounders.

There is very little flesh on a 6 oz perch, but if such fish are lying so thick as to be embarrassing, surely the thing to do is remove them in numbers.

The yellow perch of America are very little different from our own native perch. They do not reach huge proportions; (a fish over 1 lb is often referred to as a 'jumbo perch') but they are taken throughout the summer months, and through the ice in winter, by American anglers who cook them in many different ways. The perch, in America, irrespective of size (and the average is possibly little more than 4 oz) is called a pan fish. The name tells its own story. There is no catch limit in many places and anglers are *encouraged* to remove and eat these delicious little fish.

The same *could* be done in certain places in this country without any detriment to the fishing or the fish stocks. Most anglers curse loud and long when they hook suicidal perch one after the other. They do not regard them as sport fish, they do not want them in the water, and yet they still return them with loving care. I'll go along with a policy of returning *every* perch caught, where there has been a shortage and where there are hopes of fresh stocks growing on to become good sport fish; but where there are obvious surpluses I think it is stupid not to reap the harvest.

There is, and always has been, a reluctance on the part of the average housewife in this country to eat fresh water fish. I have even offered trout and sea trout to known fish lovers and my offer has been declined 'because fresh water fish taste muddy'. They don't, but freshly caught fish do need cleaning or scaling or filleting or skinning and it's easier to go to the shop and buy sea fish a couple of weeks old.

Perch, admittedly, are difficult fish to gut, gill and scale, but they are simplicity itself to fillet and skin. The diagrams in the pike chapter show how it may be done.

There is another way of removing the tough outer skin from a perch, but it is a messy business and takes longer than regular filleting.

Simply place the whole perch in a bowl, cover them with boiling water and leave them for about three minutes. The skin will 'cook' slightly and when removed from the water it will peel away from the flesh, taking spines and fins with it. *Then* the perch has to be headed, gutted and cooked whole. The impression is that a fish prepared whole provides more flesh and is less wasteful, but there is really very little in it if the filleting is carried out correctly with a sharp knife. Fillets can be taken off at the waterside or in the boat where they are being caught, and if these fillets are kept cool and moist (in cold weather only a damp cloth is necessary) they will not be an embarrassment at home.

Filleting perch (or any other fish) can really be carried out without revealing the insides; and the head and remainders are left in one piece and can be disposed of easily.

It would take a large number of fillets from 6-8 oz fish to make a man-size meal, but again I emphasise that where there is a surplus, and where it is legal to do so, it is not difficult to catch 30 or 40 perch for a family feed. I have done it many times and I hope I shall do it many more. And if the big perch return to our trout reservoirs, as they appear to be doing, I shall, perhaps, be able to do it without incurring the wrath of emotional anglers who insist, often quite wrongly, in putting everything back alive.

The following recipe is an absolute favourite of mine. I include it in this chapter because perch are exceptionally good this way. You will notice, however, that it refers to 'fish' and not essentially to 'perch', for reasons that follow.

Fillet, skin and cut fish into 'fingers'.

Roll out into meal equal quantities of Rice Krispies and potato crisps.

Dip fingers into *very hot* melted butter and roll in the meal. Lay in non-stick baking dish and bake off in a HOT oven for 10-15 minutes. *Do not* over bake. Do not use warm or cooling butter as this makes the fish greasy. Any breakfast cereal (not sweetened) will do, but Rice Krispies appear to be best.

Game fish are extremely rich cooked this way; pike, perch or grayling fillets are delicious.

Remainders are excellent eaten cold next day. Dorothy Vasconcellos of Dent, Minnesota, first put fish fillets so cooked upon my plate. They were perch, bluegills, bass, walleye and crappie, and I was impressed by the fact that they *all* tasted excellent. Individual flavours were not lost; each species was recognisable. That's the beauty of this particular recipe.

In exchange, I gave her, off the top of my head, my 'recipe' for perch in cheese sauce. After I'd told her what to do I promptly forgot, and when I was asked to repeat the recipe two years later I had no idea what I'd said. Because, you see, it doesn't matter a scrap. Basically, you lay the fish fingers in a deep dish, cover with a thick, well-seasoned cheese sauce (thick to take into account the dilution that takes place while the fish is cooking), cover with grated cheese and bake in a hot oven for thirty minutes or so. That's a simple 'au gratin' which, as every housewife knows, applies to plaice fillets, etc. Few would ever think of cooking perch or pike that way. But it doesn't end there. Try making the cheese sauce with a large chunk of Stilton (rind included). Stir half a tablespoonful of made-up English mustard into the sauce. Add a squirt of tomato purée or a teaspoonful of minced shallot, or a pinch of sage, or a hint of tabasco, or half a tin of concentrated mushroom soup, or whatever your artistic talents suggest. There's no end to the theme; it does not depend on strict weight or measurement, and each creation is just that little bit different because perch are 'versatile'.

Many years ago, two friends (Dick Walker and Peter Stone) and I spent about eight days camping and fishing on the banks of the River Tweed. We were supposed to be roach fishing but we found little real pleasure in it because the fish had yet to recover from a recent spawning.

Instead we found ourselves fishing for food. Trout were easy to catch on bait rods and we ate fish every mealtime for most of our stay. Perch were plentiful, grayling, eels and flounders added variety to our cooking and there were many occasions when firm perch fillets lay alongside pink-fleshed trout in the same pan. No-one argued regarding their allocation. The one was as acceptable as the other, and there were times when, with several kinds of fish fillets cooked together, it was almost impossible to tell one from the other. Only the flounders were distinguishable. Their slightly earthy flavour, though by no means unpleasant, was recognisable when cooked alongside perch. When cooked alone, comparison was impossible.

Of all the freshwater fish I have cooked and eaten, common perch rates very highly. It is one of our tastiest fish and yet for some strange reason is completely under-rated by the vast majority of anglers and cooks in this country.

Its flavour is recognised and appreciated in Ireland where large numbers of small perch seem to thrive, and even some of the canny Scots (most of whom only recognise the mighty salmon) enjoy perch caught from the big, clear-water lochs.

SOME PERCH RECIPES

Crispy Perch

Fillet the perch, lay in a baking dish and cover with a thick white sauce.

Roll out enough potato crisps to fill a pint jug with coarse 'meal'. (This will take a fair supply of packet crisps but do not stint them.) Oven bake the fish in the sauce and ten minutes before serving sprinkle the top with crisps to a depth of about 3/8 in. Re-heat and serve.

This recipe works well too with cream of mushroom soup substituted for the white sauce.

Both methods are improved by the addition of chopped, hardboiled egg to the sauce. A little salad cream added imparts an entirely new flavour.

Stuffed Perch

Use the boiling water skinning method to clean and prepare the fish. Mix together salt, pepper, beaten egg, cracker (or bread) crumbs, chopped parsley, dried thyme, butter and finely chopped onion. Add a little *hot* water if the mixture appears too dry; this will make it easier to handle. Place the stuffing mix into each fish and pack them tightly into a baking dish *open end* up. Dot with butter, add a very little stock or water to the bottom of the dish and bake until all is brown and tender.

Stuffed Perch fillets

Fillet the fish. Make the savoury stuffing as before and add to it the insides of several halved tomatoes. Spread the stuffing onto the perch fillets and make into rolls. Put the remaining stuffing into the scooped out tomato halves and arrange alternately in a casserole dish. Dot liberally with butter and cook in a moderate oven.

Perch Patties

Mince up raw perch fillets and mix with egg, breadcrumbs, salt, paprika, butter, finely minced onion, sage, and a little milk to make a firm mixture. Form into flat (or mini-fish-shaped) patties. Dip in beaten egg, roll in breadcrumbs, and fry in hot fat until golden brown. If there is a tendency for the onion or raw fish to remain underdone, heat under a grill, turning once, for about 10 minutes before serving.

Fish Soup (American Style)

It so happens that perch were the fish used when I first tasted this delicious and filling meal but, of course, any fish from salmon to pike would be equally fine.

Boil together perch fillets, chopped onion, a generous knob of butter, water, salt and pepper. When almost cooked add half a can of sweet corn, one large potato cut into small cubes, and about half a cup of grated cheese. Simmer *very* gently until all is tender. Stir while cooking but do not allow the potatoes to 'mash'. Before serving stir in one small tin of evaporated milk and reheat without boiling.

EELS

'DISGUSTING, SLIMY THINGS, eels,' say some.

'Perishing nuisance, they take baits intended for better fish,' say others.

'Delicious - got any more?' says the small minority.

That more or less sums up eels in the eyes of the general fishing fraternity and those who just like to eat them. Most angles curse them, a few dedicated eel hunters seek to catch monsters and often return them to the water after doing so.

I see them as a harvest to be taken by several means and while I do not seek them now as often as I once did, I neither waste nor curse them when I catch them by accident or design. They are rich food, not perhaps to everyone's taste, but oddly enough I have known people eat them, declare them delicious and still insist that they couldn't possibly eat eels.

Eels can be caught in all sorts of ways. I'm no professional, but I have worked with one and I have been amazed at some of his catches. Nets, traps and hives are all machines designed to catch eels in numbers for him. He has no eel weir like a well-organised river keeper would have, and all his eels come from a large lake complete with feeder streams and outlets incorporated, but he catches eels. How he catches eels! I have had my share of them, too, and although I could never beat him at his own game, he has allowed me to catch all I needed on rod and line.

Today it's an impossible task to catch all I need. I have so many friends who either knew all about eels at the outset, or who have been 'converted' in recent years, that I can never catch enough to satisfy every one. Every time I bring home a catch I am reminded of a dear old friend who is no longer with us.

Old Charles was a true Cockney and his favourite meal was eels in parsley sauce and mashed potatoes. His dear wife could and would have cooked them many other ways, but he would have none of it.

'Ills,' he said 'need mash and parsley'. I wouldn't agree, but I wouldn't quarrel with his statement either. Eels are good cooked almost any way, but the sad part about them is that only a few people bother to cook them, few know how to, and the remainder, as already stated, are either scared of or revolted by them.

Perhaps it is because eels resemble snakes a little. Perhaps it is because of past experiences wrestling with the tough skin. Who really knows? It is a fact, however, that eels are the most nutritious fish available. Their calorie value is horrific to those with weight problems, and it is one of the reasons why I do not actively seek them for myself any more.

Skinning an eel is not strictly necessary if it is to be jellied or steamed. I have friends who simply cut them into portions (after gutting) and cook them with the skin left intact. I believe they look more appetising when skinned and as I cook my eels in different ways, some of which entail the skin removal, I treat them all in the same way.

I have a special hook outside the shed door onto which I hang the eel through the bony part of the head. Then I cut the skin with a very sharp knife completely around the 'throat' area. This operation is tricky. Only the skin must be cut through; if the flesh is cut the head of the eel will come off and cause real problems. Next, I make a downwards cut (again through the skin only) from any point along the throat cut. This allows me to take two 'corners' of skin and ease it away from the rest of the body. From then on it is easy. Once the skin has started to peel off it only remains to take a rough towel or piece of sacking (to ensure a good grip), grasp the peeling skin firmly and pull downwards.

You do not need a special hook, of course. You can manage the job in several other ways. If you care to, you can nail the eel's head to a tree (I've done that many times) or you can have someone else hanging on to the head end while you peel off the rest. Most anglers carry a pair of forceps for hook removal. These are ideal for starting the skin to roll. You can do wonders with a pair of pliers too. All it amounts to is this: do not cut off your eel's head to kill it, and never cut off the head until the skin has been removed.

It is possible to do the whole thing on the river or lake bank and many times my friends and I have supplemented our camp ration with eels.

Skinned, split, rolled in seasoned flour and fried in shallow fat they are rich, filling, and equally delicious.

How well I remember the summer's day when Richard Walker and I fished for salmon on the Test and ended up eating eels!

We had arranged to meet a friend later and were to stay over-night in the old caravan before fishing the River Avon next morning. We had bread, butter, bacon and eggs ready for the following morning's breakfast, but it was our intention to buy meat for the evening meal on the way.

Suddenly it was 6 p.m. and we were meatless and hungry. And the shops were all closed.

I don't know who thought of it, but it was undoubtedly a good idea to go eel fishing there and then.

I caught the first one, I remember, and Richard decided to skin and clean it. His entire equipment comprised a pair of nail scissors - but he managed. Somehow he cut round the neck line, pulled off the skin and dressed out the flesh. In no time at all we had a production line going and soon we had enough.

In all we took eight eels. They were cleaned, portioned and ready to cook by the time our friend arrived. He was also very hungry, and luckily he too liked eels. We ate the lot at one sitting.

I've never taken eel fishing seriously, but I enjoy the few sessions I have each year. I fish for them mostly at night and I don't really know which part of it I enjoy most. The fight in the water, the wrestling match on the bank, or the sight of those crisp golden portions in the pan. Some of our wasteful anglers could do worse than consider that last bit.

SOME EEL RECIPES

Sautéed Eel

Skin and cut the eel into 2 in. portions. Cut each portion half way through lengthwise, open out and flatten. Roll in flour and cook in hot bacon fat. Serve with tartare sauce or plain lemon juice.

Fried Eel

Make a *thin* batter with egg, salt, pepper and flour. Dip eel portions into the batter and coat immediately with dry breadcrumbs. Leave for 10 minutes to allow the coating to become firm and dry in hot fat until crisp and golden. Use small eel portions otherwise the outside may cook too quickly, leaving the inside raw.

Jellied Eels

Boil the eels in a minimum of salted water to which a little lemon juice has been added. When cooked, remove the bones and allow the whole mass to cool and gel. In most cases the eel flesh itself will be sufficient to form the jelly, but a little gelatine may be added to ensure a firm set. If the eels are cooked with a cod's head in the same stew pan a firm set is virtually assured.

This is an old, tried and tested method, still practised today in many quarters (when cod's heads are available). The cod's head is, of course, removed from the mixture along with the eel bones.

'Jugged' Eels

Place the cleaned and skinned eels whole into a stone jar. Add a sliced onion, some chopped parsley, pepper, salt and a good knob of butter. Place the jar (covered with foil or a tight fitting lid) into a pan of cold water. Bring to the boil and cook for about $1\frac{1}{2}$ hours or until the flesh is tender. Serve with thick parsley sauce to which the cooking juices have been added.

Eel Pie (Great Grandma style)

Two lb of eels, lemon juice, a large onion, salt, pepper, nutmeg, chopped parsley, sage and onion forcemeat, thick white sauce.

Line the bottom of a pie dish with sage and onion forcemeat. Cover with lightly stewed eel portions and sprinkle with parsley, chopped onion, nutmeg and seasoning. Squeeze over the lemon juice, cover with thick white sauce, put on a puff pastry crust and cook for about 45 minutes. The pie crust may be glazed with beaten egg after it has fully risen if desired.

OTHER FISH

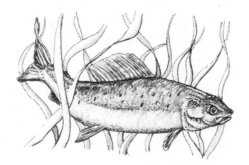

GRAYLING

The grayling, or 'Her Ladyship', 'The lady of the stream', to mention but two of her titles, really deserves a chapter to herself, but because almost all the foregoing recipes and methods of preparation apply equally to the grayling, there is little more to be said.

The adipose fin on the grayling establishes it as a member of the salmon family and that makes it, strictly speaking, a game fish. But its breeding habits are those of a coarse fish, and, in many game fishing circles, grayling are regarded as vermin.

Among the more enlightened, however, grayling are appreciated for their fine sport and subtle flavour. They are at their best in winter when they are mostly caught by intent. Summer grayling, caught by accident on trout flies, are not usually appreciated. I could write a whole chapter on grayling *fishing*, but there is little more to be said about its preparation and cooking. It is a white fleshed fish and can be poached, fried or treated in any of the ways already discussed in the chapters on trout and perch. It is reputed to have a smell or a flavour of thyme (hence its Latin name *Thymalus Thymalus*), but though I have eaten hundreds I can never remember having noticed it. Grayling are non-oily fish and while I do not know for certain how they compare with other fish regarding food value, they appear to me to be in the low calorie bracket.

Here then is a single, simple way of serving grayling without seriously exceeding a calorie limited diet.

Poach several grayling fillets in a minimum of water with a finely chopped onion. Drain and cool. Chop up together one small green pepper, a piece of cucumber and one stem of celery. Mix together equal quantities of low calorie salad cream and yoghurt and stir in the chopped vegetables. Add a little tomato purée, a pinch of salt and cayenne pepper. Stir well. Flake in the fish without breaking it into too many small portions. Serve with lettuce and tomato rings. It goes without saying, of course, that the same 'recipe' can be followed using any kind of fish. Trout are especially good this way - but, naturally, they are higher in calories.

CARP

I'll probably be hung, drawn and quartered by emotional anglers for even mentioning carp in a cookery book, but the fact remains that carp are good to eat. Where there is a surplus, there is no point in not reaping the harvest. They are delicious smoked and the American way of scoring the fillets helps render them less bony. The fillets are simply stroked with a sharp knife, making cuts both down and across. Most of the bones then disappear in the cooking. One American style of cooking carp calls for vinegar which is said to soften the bones. The carp fillets are cut into fingers, placed into an earthenware dish, covered with spiced vinegar (a mixture of pickling spice is recommended), seasoned, and then baked under a layer of sliced tomatoes for an hour. Scored carp can, of course, be fried, baked, grilled or cooked in many other ways.

I first ate a carp I had caught myself back in the early post-war years. It had been cooked by a German lady who had scaled it, simmered it whole with onions, herbs and spices, and served it flaked with 'brown butter'. I confess that I was very reluctant to taste it, but I have to admit that it was superbly cooked, and I was very impressed.

Since then I have eaten carp in the USA many, many times and I have even passed on one or two of old Izaak Walton's recipes to my American friends. We never quite got round to following the recipes in their entirety, but we did the best we could with substitutes.

Consider, for instance, trying to follow Izaak's recipe for boiled carp.

'Take a carp, alive if possible, scour him, and rub him with water and salt but scale him not. Then open him and put him with his blood and liver, which you must save when you open him, into a small pot or kettle; then take sweet marjoram, thyme, and parsley of each a handful and a sprig of rosemary and another of savory. Bind them into two or three bundles and put them to your carp with four or five onions, twenty oysters and three anchovies. Then pour upon your carp as much claret wine as will only cover him.

'Season your claret well with cloves, salt and mace, and the rinds of oranges and lemons. That done, cover your pot and set it on a quick fire till it is sufficiently boiled. Then take out the carp, lay it with the broth into the dish and pour upon it a quarter of a pound of the best fresh butter melted and beaten with half a dozen spoonfuls of the broth, the yolks of two or three eggs and some of the herbs shred. Garnish your dish with lemons and so serve it up. And much good do you.'

Follow that!

No wonder Ted Trueblood, as mentioned elsewhere in this book, reckoned an old sock would taste good if cooked in the same way. I think it would be in order to remove the carp at the end of it all and partake generously of the gravy!

GUDGEON

It is a great shame that we do not, today, follow the example of the Victorian anglers who regularly had their 'feasts of gudgeons'. These tiny fish, prolific in almost every clean river in the British

Isles, are truly delicious. They are easy to catch (sometimes much too easy) and though troublesome to prepare and cook, they can rightly be looked upon as a delicacy. The old countryman's name of 'mud gudgeon' could not be farther from the truth. Gudgeon love clear, clean, hard, gravelly-bottomed water; and there is no taste of mud in them if they are taken from such places.

I have not eaten many 'gudgeon feasts', but I recall one weekend when Richard Walker and I fished at Redmire pool for carp. A shoal of enormous gudgeon fascinated us to such an extent we caught some to eat. They averaged two ounces each and we caught thirteen of them. Headed, cleaned, dipped in seasoned flour and fried in hot butter (all the fat we had available at the time), and eaten with vinegar, and new bread and butter, those few fish made one of the most enjoyable tea-time meals I have ever eaten.

There is little more to be said about gudgeon. They are strictly fish for frying crisply like sprats and whitebait. There may be other ways of cooking them, but none could possibly be tastier than the one just described.

It is doubtful if one angler in ten thousand has ever eaten or even thought of eating gudgeon, but there, my friends, is a harvest waiting to be reaped. Try them. Organise a bankside fry-up, a gudgeon party, or a 'feast of gudgeons' and you will find yourself agreeing with me.

CRAYFISH

When streams ran clear throughout the whole British Isles there were few that did not contain fresh water crayfish. 'Miniature lobsters' is possibly as good a way of describing them as any, and they are still available where conditions allow them to thrive. Dredging, pollution, crop sprays and insecticides have taken their toll, however, and now the crayfish is a rarity. Where I could once harvest a large zinc bathful in a few hours, I am now lucky if I can find half a dozen to use for bait.

The chub of the upper Great Ouse once grew big and fat on a diet of crayfish. It was then easy to turn over a stone in the shallows and grab up a crayfish for bait. Those who had the courage (I never did) would put their hands in to arm's length and pull them out of their holes in the bank. When we wanted enough to eat, we set baited drop-nets and hauled them out covered with live crayfish every few minutes.

We would sit, my friends and I, around a camp fire with a pot of salted water bubbling continuously. We would put in a dozen or so crayfish, watch them turn lobster red, leave them to cook for a while and pick them out one at a time to eat while we talked. When the pot was empty, we replenished it, again, and again. Those 'cook-outs' were little more than snack meals, or appetisers for a later meal of perch, pike or steak, but what snacks they were! And what colourful decorations these deep red creatures made to dishes of salmon or trout.

They tasted excellent too when sautéed in butter and served with rice and peppers, and it is a tragedy that stocks have disappeared completely from so many clear streams.

Where they still exist and are not an endangered species, they breed quickly and in profusion. Only the large ones should be taken and they should be put into boiling salted water as quickly as possible.

The tail segment and the big claws are the only edible portions. Eating crayfish is rather like eating walnuts; it takes longer to extract the edible parts than it does to eat them. By taking the tail 'fin', twisting it and pulling carefully, the narrow gut can usually be pulled clear in one piece. It doesn't matter much if it breaks, however; the tail portion can be halved and the offending piece removed if desired.

OUTDOOR COOKING

CAMPFIRES AND BARBECUES

When I think of outdoor cooking I am reminded of the days when, as children, we used to catch fish or shoot rabbits and then light a campfire in order to cook and eat them. Some, indeed most, of our finished products should have been completely inedible. They were scorched or downright soot-blackened on the outside, raw in the middle, smoky and, as likely as not, covered in grit. But we fooled ourselves into believing we enjoyed eating them. Perhaps, on reflection, we actually *did* enjoy them. We used up a lot of energy before we finally achieved our aim and I believe that the old saying about hunger being the best sauce applied to us. We were always hungry when we roamed the fields and woods.

Perhaps the fact that those memories have stayed with me all my life has turned me into a competent outdoor cook, and while going out into the wilds to practise 'survival' techniques is not everyone's idea of fun, there are many ways of preparing and cooking food outside that will turn kitchen-prepared meals into 'also rans'.

Outdoor cooking does not necessarily have to be done over a smoky camp fire out in the wilderness. It can be done in a small garden, using modern barbecue units or smokers, but there is still something to be said for camp fire cookery and this book would not be complete without some mention of it.

If you have not crawled out of a frost-covered sleeping bag at dawn, walked down to the stream and caught tiny troutlets, returned to camp and cooked them with bacon in a thick iron skillet, and if you have not savoured the smell of wood smoke mingling with that of freshly made coffee and crisp bacon, you have not yet lived! If you have not placed an iron grid over the embers of a log fire and watched the juices from thick steaks splutter into flames that lick around them to form a crisp, charcoal seal, you have a treat yet to come when you taste steaks cooked as they should be cooked.

Steaks, of course, have little to do with game and fish cookery, but the principles are the same, and whether you use a simple campfire or a modern barbecue unit, you can produce similar results with rabbit, venison, pigeon, hare and other game. There are also ways and means of cooking fish on open fires that are simple in the extreme.

The main problem regarding outdoor cooking in this country, of course, is that if you plan an outdoor party it's a racing certainty that it will then rain solidly for two whole days. That's *one* of the sad and dark sides.

The other is that most outdoor cooking ventures are tackled by people who always seem to be in a hurry. Food is murdered over lukewarm coals, charcoal briquettes are not given time to redden, meat is removed from heat because it looks as if it is about to set fire, and is often eaten smelling or tasting of the fuel to start the fire at the outset.

It matters little what kind of game you are cooking over an open fired unit provided it is *tender* game. Old cock pheasants or wild goose 'leaders', with spurs that betray their age, should not be subjected to this kind of cooking. Their final destination should be the stewpot or casserole dish, and they will not taste any the worse for that. Secondly, do not be afraid of heat when outdoors. Lean meat can be brushed with some kind of butter or fat before placing over the coals, and there are many kinds of barbecue sauce that can be brushed on during the cooking. One or two such sauces are described elsewhere in this book. But sauce or no sauce, *do not* put the meat over the coals and turn it over two seconds later because it appears to be burning. Leave it, then when you're absolutely sure it is burned to a crisp, leave it a little longer. When did you ever see a piece of meat of any kind begin to burn to a crisp in a few seconds? It's impossible. But by fearing the worst and turning a portion of game, chicken, steak or any kind of meat every few seconds you are actually ruining the outdoor cooking process.

Let it cook on one side. Let the underside seal itself and maintain all its nutrition. *Do not* keep turning it and letting all those lovely goodies drip into the fire. Three minutes seems an awfully long time when you're watching a portion of prime meat 'burn', but that's about how long it should be left before it is turned. It depends, of course, to a large extent on the size, thickness and leanness of the game being cooked, but both sides should be sealed well. During the final cooking stages, it may be turned just as often as you wish. Those opening moves are the important ones.

You do not need charcoal. You can achieve the same results from the embers of a wood fire, but soft woods such as pine are not recommended.

Where a camp fire is strictly the only means of cooking and where no utensils or grids are available, *all* kinds of fish, game and wildfowl can be cooked in foil. It is an absolutely infallible way of cooking anything from a pheasant to a jacket potato, and it's a superb way of cooking fish of all kinds. Again all kinds of variations can be added to provide subtle flavour changes.

All you do is wrap up whatever you're going to cook into a parcel of kitchen foil. Then (the important part) wrap it again with one more layer.

Let us assume, for the sake of demonstration, that you have a rabbit for cooking outside. Here is how I would prepare the meal, and it is how I have done it many times in Britain, America and Australia. Cut up the rabbit and lay the portions on a square of kitchen foil. (Cut off any jagged or protruding bones to prevent the foil from puncturing). Cut up the liver, heart and kidneys into small pieces leaving the fat that surrounds the kidneys intact. Add about $\frac{1}{2}$ lb of streaky pork or a few dabs of lard or white fat and a chopped onion.

Sprinkle with salt, black pepper and mixed herbs. Wrap it all up into a tight package. Now wrap up *that* package into another one and toss it into the fire after the flames have died down a little and the embers are red. Keep the fire going by adding a little fuel now and then. I know you'll be thinking that in five minutes the meat will be a blackened mess, but you have my word for it that it will *not*. Leave it for at least half an hour, turning it over occasionally. The moisture inside will prevent burning and the steam generated will cook the meat to tender perfection. And now, you see, here's the real joy of such cooking. Shake off the ash from the outer layer of foil and unwrap it carefully. The inner wrapper should now be perfectly clean and free from ash or grit. Open it up, use it as a plate, eat the contents with your fingers and forget the washing up.

During some of the electricity cuts we have experienced from time to time, I have used this method to cook game, potatoes and vegetables over an ordinary coal fire indoors (I am old-fashioned enough still to enjoy an open fire) and I can claim, in all truth, that the results were perfect every time.

And, if anyone has a mind to find out what this simple but effective kind of cooking is all about, they can practise it on an indoor fire before venturing out into the great outdoors.

Barbecue units with meat cooking on the top grid can of course also be used for foil wrap cooking. Corn cobs, potatoes, and so on can be cooked in the coals while the meats are being prepared.

There was a time when I thought the American style outdoor barbecue unit was unbeatable, but since visiting Australia, where the principle is slightly different, I have changed my mind.

The American unit exposes the meat to the glowing coals and with starter fuel and charcoal bricks as part of the deal, it is, to some extent, an 'artificial' set-up.

The Australian unit, which can be brick built or made from a half-sectional oil drum, comprises a $\frac{1}{4}$ in. thick mild steel hot plate beneath which a roaring log fire is built up. The plate heats up, burning off all the grease left from any previous meal and then, when it has cooled sufficiently, it is smeared with a little oil or fat and the meats are laid on top. Alongside the meats go onions, sliced tomatoes, cut bread rolls, sausages and so on, and underneath, in the embers, go the foil wrapped potatoes.

Rabbit, so cooked in Australia, would not be considered edible without the essential litre of ice cold beer to help it down; and the *correct* and *only* way of telling if the hot plate is at the right temperature for cooking is to pour onto it a spot or two, of the said beer. If it disappears in a cloud of steam it's too hot; if it stays long enough to begin to run, the temperature is just right.

It goes without saying that trout, sea trout, and other fish can be cooked using the double wrap foil method. Fish takes less time to cook but the same principles apply. Sauces, spices, seasonings, lemon juice, butter and vinegar, are a few of the many additives that can be used to enhance the flavour of every common fish.

'HOLES IN THE GROUND' AND 'HAY BOXES'

Not every sportsman spends long days and nights out in the open or under canvas in search of fish or game, but there are times when it makes sense to form a base camp, whether it is tent, boathouse, fishing hut or caravan, in order to spend more time pursuing his or her favourite quarry. The carp fisher, the specimen hunter who needs long hours to contact his fish, does so almost every weekend during the summer season. That is a stay-put exercise, generally speaking; both camp and fishing pitch are one and the same. Cooking can be done as and when fancy dictates.

The angler who fishes remote hill lochs or streams for trout, sea trout or the occasional salmon may, however, find it necessary to walk many miles in the course of the day. It may even take half a day to reach the fishing area, and it is then that the ability to enjoy the day, before returning to a good meal at base camp later, becomes important.

I do not wish to dwell upon the survival theme, but it is worth remembering that hill mists can descend upon unwary travellers and long walks across peaty moors to distant lochs should not be undertaken lightly. There is no point in loading up with unnecessary food and equipment but it pays to anticipate a possible emergency. All I will say is 'be prepared, equip yourself so that an enforced overnight stay is not the end of the world, and make provision for a hot meal if and when you return to base late at night'. The number one priority, as I see it, is that you should be able to light a fire. We may all have different ideas on 'survival' food, but none of that is of much use if it cannot be cooked. For that reason alone I carry a *double supply* of matches that are not likely to get wet. I still have vivid memories of a cold dawn spent looking at six raw bacon rashers and a box of damp matches.

Fires comprised mainly of damp heather or similar herbage do not start easily even with good dry matches, but a small stub of candle will burn long enough to get the most stubborn fuel started.

That's about all there is to it. All the gear I carry can be crammed into a fishing waistcoat. There's even room for a lightweight waterproof jacket or sheet in the back pocket, and I find the waistcoat more comfortable and convenient than a haversack or shoulder pack.

You can carry as much food around as you deem necessary and it makes sense to view each situation on its merits, but with a few bare essentials it's possible to survive and maintain a feeling of true contentment without having to rough it more than necessary.

I have been fortunate in that I have been able to spend long days (even weeks) in remote places in search of fish, and I have become adept at making the most of available resources. Apart from trout, caught and cooked on the spot by the foil parcel method already described, I have enjoyed pike, perch, eels, grayling and, the greatest delicacy of all, small sea trout or herling in these wild and desolate places.

In the USA and Canada I have spent weeks catching bass, bluegills and other edible fish in temperatures of 100°F plus, without ever seeing another human being apart from my immediate companions. Up in the Outer Hebrides I have done exactly the same thing in temperatures considerably lower. In the Welsh mountains, Scottish Highlands and Cumberland fells I have, in all honesty, foregone opportunities to fish traditionally for salmon and sea trout. Instead I have walked and climbed for miles in search of small trout for the pan and for immediate cooking on the bank of the water from which they were caught.

I have 'roughed it' in the Oregon desert, the Rocky Mountains of Wyoming, and Montana; I have spent time in the bush country and the Canadian wilderness because I love and respect all wide open spaces. I do not tell you this to prove that I am a well-travelled veteran, but rather to prove that the formula for *enjoyable survival* is the same the world over.

I won't tell you what to carry in the way of food while you are away from base camp, but I will tell you of a good idea for your return meal. It has to be prepared before you leave and it cooks itself while you are away. It cannot go wrong, it cannot burn and it *will* be hot and nourishing, no matter how many hours you are away.

I refer, of course, to 'Dutch oven' or 'hole-in-the-ground' cooking.

A Dutch oven is a weighty cast-iron stew pot into which are piled all the essentials for a nourishing stew. Let us not go into details. Beef, mutton, rabbit, hare, venison, who cares? With onions, carrots (dried pulse vegetables if you like), rice or barley, tomato purée, meat extract, seasoning and/or anything else you would or could put in an ordinary stew (including potatoes which you may leave whole) added, and brought to the boil for half an hour on the camp fire, you are ready for action.

Alongside the fire dig a hole about 2 ft deep, scrape half the camp fire into it, place the Dutch oven on top and scrape the rest of the fire on to it.

Then fill in the hole with the excavated earth, and that's it. Mark the spot, dig up the treasure 6, 8 or 10 hours later and enjoy one of the best feeds you ever tasted.

Not everyone has a Dutch oven, of course. In fact it's highly unlikely that there are many in the U.K. but an ordinary heavy duty saucepan or an old pressure cooker will serve the same . The Dutch oven has a lipped lid which holds the burning embers on top and prevents ash from falling into the pot, but almost the same effect can be achieved by using a seal of kitchen foil on an ordinary saucepan with a fairly tight-fitting lid.

It's also possible to cook meat or game wrapped in foil by the same method. Scrape out a shallow trough and light the camp fire in the depression. After breakfast, *treble* wrap the meat or game to be cooked, scrape away most of the fire and place the package in the depression. Cover with the fire embers and pile earth on top to retain the heat. This meal will be cooked on return to base, but it may have cooled sufficiently to require warming up in a pan.

Hay box cookery speaks for itself, of course. Originally hay was used to retain heat. It is still possible to dig a large hole, line it with tightly packed hay, bring a stew or pot roast to the boil for about 20 minutes and transfer it, while still boiling, to the hay hole. If well covered with more hay and topped up with soil, the food will continue cooking for about 6-8 hours.

Once it begins to cool off, however, it will quickly sour. It should not be left covered for more than about 8 hours. The same principle was later used with hay lined boxes. Later still, with better insulating materials and 'dixies' made to fit tightly into boxes with tightly sealed lids, the army learned to cook its meals on the move.

It is possible today to produce the same result by using a pressure cooker and transferring it at pressure point to a large box containing newspapers and modern insulating granules. It works; I have proved it during power cuts.

I may have given the impression here that the Dutch camp oven is used exclusively for hole-in-the-ground cookery but nothing could be farther from the truth. It is, in its own right, a superb utensil that will serve as a skillet, griddle, roast oven, stewpot, or baking oven. Its flanged lid keeps out ash and dust and the lip which surrounds it allows hot coals to rest on it and provide top heat. Thus it may be used to cook almost anything in as grand a style as any gas or electric oven.

To bake a damper or sourdough loaf, as described in chapter 2, the oven needs to be warmed over the camp fire first. Then some of the fire is raked to one side and the oven, containing the dough, is placed on the hot ground, the lid replaced and covered with hot, glowing embers and the all-round heat is controlled by placing a few more embers around the base. It is impossible to say how long or how many coals it takes to bake a particular product but the principle is the same for everything. Top heat and bottom heat ensure all-round heat and although the tight seal of the Dutch oven is an advantage, it is possible to bake bread, cakes and pies as well as roasts and casseroles by applying the principle to makeshift utensils. I have cooked sourdough and roast rabbit in an old iron pot with a discarded non-stick frying pan used as a lid. The pan has been filled with hot coals and, although some heat has escaped, the Dutch oven principle has always been successful. It should be pointed out that thin-walled pots or pans are not likely to prove satisfactory. They become too hot too quickly and do not retain the necessary heat.

One other simple method of cooking trout out of doors comes to mind as a result of my association with Kingfisher Television. I took part in several programmes associated with outdoor sports and during one of them, I remembered and demonstrated the Irish method of cooking trout in newspaper. It is simplicity itself.

After gutting and gilling, the trout is sprinkled inside and out with salt and pepper and a squirt of lemon juice (or vinegar) inside along with a nut or two of butter.

The trout is then wrapped in newspaper (use a whole newspaper one sheet at a time for best results) and left in water to become *completely saturated.* This is important! I once watched a self-styled expert demonstrate the method on T.V. She wrapped the fish in one sheet of paper, sprinkled it with water and popped it in the oven! We never saw the end result but it was easy enough to guess!

The whole principle of the method involves the creation of steam by extreme heat. The wet parcel is simply tossed into a blazing fire where it slowly dries out and cooks the trout to perfection. I have never had problems with the method and I have cooked fish of all sizes up to and including a 5lb. salmon. Obviously bigger fish need longer cooking and it is advisable then to use more paper. When the parcel begins to scorch and burn it may be fairly assumed that a modest fish is cooked. Any doubts regarding bigger specimens may be resolved by turning the parcel frequently and trickling on more water to moisten it further. When the parcel is unwrapped the skin comes away with the newspaper leaving the flesh exposed.

This leaves one more kind of outdoor cooking - smoking, which is somewhat different.

SMOKING

Smoking is, in many respects, a vague process. I find it hard to believe that it can ever be reduced to an exact science although it has been attempted. Now I know that it is very much like a regular cooking process and that there is room for improvisation as often as not.

"No two days or nights are exactly the same," said the foreman smoker at Messrs. Barnetts of Frying Pan Alley, who are renowned for their smoked salmon.

"You have to use your own discretion according to the prevailing conditions."

Much the same statement was made to me when I visited the big smoke chimneys of Messrs. Robinsons at Fleetwood. "Sometimes the wind blows at night here and we have to come in and regulate things," said foreman Ken Summers. "You have to use your loaf."

There was a time when I tried to find out facts and figures in the belief that I could learn the secrets of smoking. I believed it to be a highly secretive process and that great skills were involved. I was convinced that I would never be able to produce smoked salmon, trout or sea trout to compare with those processed by the professionals. Now I know I can. I have learned by experience and I have studied the great differences between hot smoking and cold smoking. I have learned that hot smoking is, in fact, cooking in smoke and that a smoke flavour can be applied to all kinds of fish, eels, game, poultry, wild fowl or whatever by the hot smoking process.

If we recognise this fact and accept that, unlike cold smoking (of which more later) hot smoking does little, if anything to preserve the product but simply cooks it in another way, we shall better understand the whole business.

I remember once in Arkansas we hot smoked a 10 lb Coho salmon and a 10 lb carp together. Both were soaked overnight in a brine solution made up of salt, brown sugar, molasses and water. The wood smoke was made from hickory chips and the fish were kept ticking over nicely for 12 hours. At the outdoor party that evening I am certain that no-one knew one from the other. Several times we were complimented on the smoked salmon by someone digging into a chunk of smoked carp - all of which helps to prove that hot smoking can improve the flavour of almost any fish.

But not only that. Young rabbit, pheasant, even sausages, can be improved by hot smoking. And the beauty of it all is that it's almost impossible to spoil them in the process. The only error can come in the timing. There is a chance that the meat may be under-cooked, but all you need do in these circumstances is put it back in and repeat the process.

Over-cooking tends to dry out fish, but, like many other kinds of cooking, hot smoking requires no strict weighing, measuring or timing at certain temperatures. You can treat it as technically as you wish and for consistent results it pays to do so but the real pleasure lies in playing around with different solutions and woods. That's when it could be regarded as an art rather than a science. For as long as you do not become involved in 'recipes' results will differ every time, but the one is just as likely to be as delicious as the other. That's part of the fun; only a degree of common sense is necessary.

One of the finest meals I ever had was ribs of beef cooked outdoors over hickory and apple smoke. It was in Oklahoma and, if I remember rightly, the smoker was made from a huge oil drum and the smoke was generated, not by sawdust or chips, but by smouldering logs. The only reason, as I see it, for using sawdust is to prevent an outbreak of flame. This is important in cold smoking, of course, but not so vital in hot smoking or 'smoke roasting'.

The 'fire box' of the outdoor smoke oven in Oklahoma was such that the heat could be generated by the burning logs and controlled by a crude but effective damper which ensured that they smouldered slowly without flame.

Provided the difference between cold smoking and hot is understood, the field is wide open to experiment. Without putting too fine a point on it, the colder the smoke, the longer the process takes *and* the longer the finished product will keep afterwards. That's a generalisation, but it isn't far off the mark.

The American idea of putting an electric hotplate (with heat-proof wiring) inside an old refrigerator and placing on top of it an iron skilletful of oak chips, works well enough until the temperature hits zero. Then the metal exterior cools the inside too quickly for the food to cook.

Up in Minnesota I once enjoyed sharing in a great catch of tulibee. These are white fish of the Cisco family and run to about 3 lb. We caught them through 40 in. of ice while the outside temperature was in the region of 30° below zero *Fahrenheit.*

They were hot smoked outside in the same conditions. The smoker was an old refrigerator and the smoke was made from cherry wood. Extra heat was generated by red hot barbecue charcoal in a biscuit tin on the lower shelf, and the American outdoorsman who cooked them used his own favourite salt solution which added to the flavour of these great delicacies.

Small, portable smokers that work extremely well on methylated spirit fuel are available in Britain. Most tackle shops sell them and they come with a supply of oak sawdust which is reputed to be the beat smoke-producing wood. These smokers are adequate for fish up to a couple of pounds and they will handle fish cutlets or fillets also. Despite the oak sawdust that comes with these units, it would appear that many other hard woods are also suitable. Cherry, hawthorn and apple are three that have passed the test. Beech is said to be good but I cannot speak from experience. Mixtures of several hard woods can make subtle differences to the flavour of fish or game and only soft woods like pine are likely to ruin good food.

Outdoor friends of mine in America have told me tales of smokers made on site from available natural materials. Log constructions were covered with leaves, fern and other herbage to retain the smoke. They were built as an essential part of camp life during several weeks' stay in bush or mountain country where it was necessary to keep fish without refrigeration. Some say that is how smoking originated in the USA. The Indians, they say, dried their fish and meat in order to keep it longer. Fire smoke was used to keep away the flies and it was found that the flavour was improved by the smoke from different woods. True or not, it *is* feasible. In all probability those same discoveries have been made in other parts of the world throughout its whole history.

It is unlikely that the average angler or his family would need a unit much larger than the popular commercial portable model, but if anyone is interested and sufficiently technically here is how to make one capable of hot smoking a big fish.

Take an old refrigerator and remove all the plastic, rubber seal and insulation. Put an electric hot plate inside via a small drilled hole in the side. Use a heat resisting flex. On top of the hot plate set an old, thick, metal pan and load it with sawdust. It takes some time to heat up but once the smoke is circulating the cooking process begins.

Old damp sacking can be placed over any wide gaps to prevent a mass escape of smoke but some ventilation is necessary to ensure complete circulation. Do not put the fish in until the smoke has begun to appear. Hang the fish on hooks or lay it on wire trays to ensure that it is smoke-treated all over. Try to maintain the heat between 150°F minimum and 200°F maximum. The only way this can be achieved accurately, of course, is by installing a thermometer through a small drilled hole in the top of the unit.

Before smoking your fish, soak it in your favourite brine solution for several hours (overnight if you wish) or sprinkle it with dry salt just beforehand. As I explained earlier, results will differ if you experiment, but just for starters here is a good basic brine mix.

Add ¾ lb of salt and 6 oz of brown sugar to one gallon of water. Sprinkle in a little pepper, and if you like add a few bay leaves. When the fish has been well soaked, wash off the brine and dry with a cloth. Then proceed with the hot smoking method. Smaller fish should be well done in about 2-4 hours, but big 10-20 pounders will need much longer - say 10-12 hours. The actual time depends on outside conditions and all sorts of other factors, but there is no reason for not inspecting and watching its progress. Apart from dealing with a big batch of fish, however, this kind of smoker will not do anything that one of the small portable units can do. For single, small fish the portable unit is still superior.

There is nothing very difficult about cold smoking especially if we remember that a smoker is really only a chimney of sorts.

Fish that has been salt-cured and hung in a chimney (which can be made from a drain pipe, a dustbin, or an old refrigerator casing) can be improved by smoking, but it is essential to understand that the smoking procedure has little to do with the preserving of the fish. If we accept that any fish treated either in brine or dry salt will be, to all intents and purposes, "cured", the smoking process will be better understood.

Smoking, after salt curing, may dry out the flesh a little more but, in fact, it serves largely to impart the smoky flavour. That is basically what cold smoking is all about and if we try to forget the keeping qualities of brined and smoke-dried fish we will, perhaps, be able to dispense with some of the mystery. At the end of the cold-smoking process we are still going to eat fish which remains more or less raw but which is free from bacteria because the salting has already taken care of those.

Firstly, we have to fillet the big trout and some experience is necessary here. Two slabs may be taken from the fish, however, simply by cutting along both sides of the back bone. This will leave a few bones in but they can be removed from the end product.

The skin should be left on and the fillets covered in dry salt. The amount is not critical and there are no laid-down quantities, but it takes a couple of pounds or so of rock salt (NOT table salt) to cover a couple of big fillets. Believe me, the amount of salt is not too important as long as the flesh is covered. After about six hours of salting, during which time a great deal of moisture will be drawn from the fish, the salt has to be washed off completely. Then, it is vital for the slabs to be dried until a pellicle or sheen appears. This process cannot be hurried and it really does not matter if it is allowed to continue overnight in a cool larder or outhouse. The slabs can then be hooked and hung in the chimney where a cool draught of smoke from smouldering hardwood sawdust for twelve hours or so will complete the process.

It is important to remember that the fish is not being cooked at this stage but that the smoky flavour and rich colour will increase the longer the process continues. Longer smoking will make the product dryer and ensure longer keeping qualities at a normal refrigerator temperature. It is, however, perfectly safe to portion and deep freeze the smoked fish until required. A wisp of blue smoke passing up the chimney and past the hanging fish is to be preferred to masses of grey and acrid fumes. There is no need to hurry and it does not matter if the fire goes out overnight. You simply re-light it again next day.

An old iron skillet or bowl heated over a gas burner to start the sawdust smoking saves a great deal of firelighting and makes for a more controllable system. Once the sawdust is fired, the gas burner may be turned off. The smoke should not be hot in the chimney.

If it feels warm to the hand, the fire should be withdrawn briefly and if it is possible to "relay" the smoke through a pipe before it reaches the chimney, so much the better.

These are vague instructions because the whole business is vague. It is not an exact science but a fun process which requires simple common sense. It is virtually impossible to ruin anything!

Extremes of hot and cold weather do not help the cold smoke process. On a hot summer's day the chimney may heat up more than necessary and it is then advisable to apply the smoke at night while keeping the fish cool by day.

In frosty conditions it is just possible that the fish may freeze and miss out on the smoke process. This is easily controlled by increasing the smoke heat.

If asked to outline the most important aspects of a cold smoking process, I would suggest that the forming of the dry pellicle is vital. Unless the fish has dried to this point it will soften in the smoke and probably fall off its retaining hooks. There is no more depressing sight than a slab of trout shrivelling in a panful of ashes!

I would agree, perhaps, with my American friends who suggest that a thermometer to maintain a temperature not higher than 90oF is worthy of consideration. And I would insist that there is never any need to hurry a cold smoking process. Big fish need longer salting, longer drying and longer smoking and what is not completed today may be left until tomorrow or the next day.

While I prefer the dry salt method there is much to be said for experimenting with different brine solutions. Many Americans use a mixture of one gallon of water to 1 lb. of salt, ½ lb. of brown sugar and a pinch of saltpetre. They insist that the brined fish should not be washed off in between times but left to dry out thoroughly before smoking. I prefer, nevertheless, to wash off all surplus brine before drying. I have found it advisable in the past, especially when a strong brine has been used.

I should also perhaps point out that it is possible to create smoke without a gas or electric heat source. My own preference, as a refinement to my brick built chimney (which is an extension of a plate type barbecue) is a gas ring fuelled by bottled gas but I have made do with a few sticks of kindling or a few charcoal briquettes.

In these circumstances a fine sawdust is preferable to chips or shavings since the last-mentioned do not always pack down tightly enough to continue burning.

Once the fish is processed it should keep for a couple of weeks or more. The stronger the brine (up to a point) and the longer the smoking process takes, the longer the finished product should keep.

Both hot and cold smoked fish can provide the basis for a number of tasty, made-up dishes, some of which follow. In the meantime they may be tackled just as they are - with relish!

Smoked Fish recipes

1. Bring smoked fish (any kind) to the boil quickly in unsalted water. Remove, lay in an ovenproof dish, sprinkle with black pepper and a little finely chopped parsley. Barely cover with full cream milk, add a tablespoonful or so of double cream (optional) and dot all over with nuts of butter. Bake in a moderate oven for about 30 minutes and serve.

2. Cook smoked fish briefly in milk, flake off bones and lay the flakes in a casserole dish. Make a thin white sauce from the milk and add cream, beaten egg yolks and paprika. Pour sauce over fish flakes and grill quickly.

3. Boil long-grain rice in salted water until it is barely cooked. Refresh under a cold tap. Cook smoked fish briefly in water and flake off bones. Mix it lightly with rice. Add a pinch of cayenne pepper, some very finely chopped mushrooms, and finely chopped hard-boiled eggs. Cover with a thin creamy white sauce, and bake off in a hot oven for about 20 minutes. The foregoing can also be served as a cold salad dish, without the addition of the white sauce and without further cooking. Garnish with parsley and shrimps if desired.

Fish that has been subjected to the hot smoke process really needs little more than a plate from which to eat it, but it can be presented in many different ways to avoid boredom.

I could fill this book with smoked fish recipes alone, but once again I suggest you try and dream up some of your own.

Here are a few thoughts of my own to get you started. They are all tried and tested.

Take an oval fish plate and fill the centre with flaked smoked fish. Down the centre lay a row of thinly sliced lemon and cucumber placed to overlap alternately. It takes a little time but it looks very professional. Surround the fish with shredded lettuce leaves, sliced tomato, watercress, shelled prawns and chopped hard-boiled egg. Squeeze a little lemon juice over the whole dish and serve with thinly sliced brown bread and butter. The same dish can be served with very finely chopped white cabbage instead of the lettuce, and a coleslaw dressing can be added if desired.

In the process of trimming, filleting and smoking trout, there will inevitably be left-overs. They should not be wasted.

The bones from which the fillets have been taken should be boiled in a minimum of water and the flesh flaked off them into a separate dish. Keep the stock. Later, when the smoked fish is trimmed to remove fins and possibly dried-up tail ends, these remainders should be placed in the stock along with any left-over smoked skin.

If, at this stage, there are any left-over fish portions of any kind available, they too should be cooked in the stock which should then be strained through a sieve. When all skin, fins and inedible fish scraps have been removed, the remaining edible fish should be put into a food processor and thoroughly blended.

Then it should be added to the stock along with an equal (more or less) weight of butter, a little mixed mustard, a squirt of tomato purée and a pinch of cayenne pepper and brought to the boil.

The consistency should be similar to that of a flour batter but it is not critical. After the mix has cooled it should be put into small tubs and left to set. The resultant pâté has to be tasted to be believed. It is made entirely of left-over scraps and yet, I swear, I have been offered large sums of money to produce it on a regular basis. What can be achieved by using the whole fish may only be described as "work"! In recent years I have been tossed trout and salmon weighing up to 11 lb. with the instructions to 'turn it into pâté for me please'.

I have since called a halt to such endeavours but I am still asked regularly for samples and, up to a point, I am happy to accept such requests as compliments.

Obviously there is a case here for experimenting with the more easily processed hot-smoked fish and for various herbal additions to improve the basic flavour.

SOME MORE MIXED DISHES

Game Pie - Hot
1. Trim meat from any mixture of game and cut into dice.
Pressure cook the remaining carcases until the meat falls off and a
concentrated stock remains.
2. Toss the meat dice in seasoned flour and brown in hot shallow
fat. Brown diced onions, carrots and mushrooms in same fat.
Cover all with the stock, and cook slowly until the meat is tender
and the liquid thick. Season to taste.
3. Place in a large pie dish, cover with short crust pastry (made
from pure lard), brush with diluted beaten egg and bake at 400°F.
(This dish is improved by the addition of *lean* ham or pork at stage
2.)

Game Pie - Cold
1. Repeat stage 1, cutting the dice extra small.
2. Add ¼ lb of not-too-lean pork and ¼ lb wholemeal breadcrumb (soaked and squeezed) to each 1 lb of game meat. Add liberal dashes of salt, pepper and sage.
3. Pack into a pie crust paste (hot-water paste for raised pies or short paste for tinned pies).
Bake for 15 minutes or so at 450°F. Egg glaze and then lower temperature to 300oF for 1½ hours.
Add 1 oz of gelatine to 1 pint of the reduced stock and, when the pie has cooled, pour this through the steam-escape hole in the pastry and allow to set.

The next recipe, being a little offbeat by British standards, needs perhaps a slightly longer explanation. My version of it contains mixed game of any kind, but I give it its odd name because more often than not I make it with rabbit.

Chili-Con-Coney
It is said that chili came from Mexico and found its way to Texas and the southern states of America early this century. Its name derives, so we are told,, from the hot chili peppers used in its preparation. The Americans added meat to the dish and the name chili-con-carne (chili with meat) was born. The meat could only have been minced beef (or hamburger as the Americans call it) and the chili served in the USA today usually contains beef of some kind.
There are many variations and since 1969 I have used a number of basic recipes substituting game of one kind or other for the beef. Here is one of them.
The ingredients are: 1 lb meat from any available game, 2 large onions (finely chopped), 1 Large tin of tomatoes, ½ dessertspoonful of salt, 2 green peppers (finely chopped), 1 level dessert spoonful of chili powder and 1 large tin of beans.

The last ingredient presents a problem because the recipe calls for kidney beans. If tinned kidney beans are not readily available, cooked butter beans, haricot beans or a tin of commercial baked beans in tomato sauce can be substituted. I prefer the tinned variety for convenience.

The meat should be tossed and browned in a frying pan along with the onions and peppers. Then it should be cooked slowly with the tomatoes and a little stock or water. Bay leaves and/or cloves can be added, and so can a hint of tabasco sauce.

When the meat is completely tender (after about an hour) the beans should be added and everything brought to the boil again. Stock or water may have to be added to keep all moist if the dish is cooked on top of the stove; if it is cooked in the oven this is not quite so important.

That, with as many variations as you can imagine, is basic chili and if you find you like it you can really go to town with game, rabbit, pigeon and wild fowl substituted for the beef. You can make it richer, meatier or thicker. You can serve it as a 'starter soup' on a cold day or as a main dish for a hungry hunter.

I know that I never tire of rabbit because I have learned so many ways of preparing it and I think that what I refer to as 'Chili-con-Coney' takes a lot of beating.

I do not mince the rabbit, but trim it from the bones and dice it finely. I pressure cook the bones to produce a rich stock and add this to the other ingredients as they cook. If you do no more than follow the above recipe, replacing the beef with chopped rabbit, you will have a meal that really does represent an excellent change from traditional rabbit fare. But you can do more. You can use any kind of game or venison. You can add macaroni or pasta of some kind. You can increase the tomato taste by a squirt or two of tomato purée. You can, as you might do with a regular curry, add chutney, apples, raisins, desiccated coconut, or whatever else takes your fancy. The result is perhaps not strictly chili, but it *is* good.

You can grate cheddar cheese into or over the dish, or you can sprinkle it with parmesan.

You can (as one of my American friends does) make 'biscuits' (which are really dumplings as we know them) and oven-bake them in the bubbling chili. The biscuits rise to the surface and the tops take on a crisp golden crust which is truly delicious. The ordinary plain scone mixture known to every housewife in the land, with the sugar omitted and a couple of ounces of grated cheese added, will also make 'floating biscuits' with a difference.

Burgoo

I always regarded burgoo as an Indian word meaning porridge. That was its British Army meaning at any rate. But in America it has another meaning - it is a game and vegetable broth, with no holds barred.

Country communities in the USA are closely bound by church groups and other social gatherings, and one of their ways of raising funds is to organise an outdoor burgoo party. We are not exactly talking of the Feeding of the Five Thousand here, but we are talking about 50 gallons (at least) of mixed game, meats, and vegetables. It is traditionally cooked over an open fire and every conceivable item of edible foodstuff goes into it. It is not made to a recipe but to an accumulation. The burgoo is cooked all night long, stirred with wooden paddles by the menfolk, and sold by the bowlful next day at one or other type of outdoor gathering. It needs no thickening; as the meats and vegetables, corn and other items, cook and swell the liquid thickens, the air fills with an aroma of good food and the end product, though never the same twice running, is always excellent.

Moose meat, venison, rabbit, squirrel, pheasant, quail, and many other kinds of hunted game (no beef or farm produced meat is used) go into the pot. Barley, rice, corn, tomatoes, potatoes, cucumbers, peppers, squash, onions, turnips, shredded cabbage (I could go on, of course) are all used. Nothing is wasted.

The approach of a new shooting season prompts me now, in the light of USA experiences, to have a final burgoo deep-freeze clearance. Charles Bowen and I did just that in Illinois a few years ago. His freezer was loaded with oddments of game. His garden was full of surplus vegetables and so we lit up the big barbecue unit outside his home. We set a 5-gallon container on it and put into it no less than fourteen kinds of vegetables and five kinds of game meat. Charles stirred all day long, and I prepared and brought out the meat and vegetables as and when they were ready.

The result was an excellent supper that filled six hungry people to capacity and a dozen or more quart containers were put into the deep freeze for midday soup meals later.

I have never gone quite to that length on my own, but when I have a surplus of game and need more freezer space, I make American-style burgoo. It doesn't last long!

COUNTRY WINES

I could, if I so wished, write a book about country wines, but I would simply be repeating what so many others have written in the past. I would find it hard not to use recipes already popular with country wine makers countrywide and, in order to do the subject justice, I would have to become involved in a scientific study. The truth is that the manufacture of wines today is a strict science. No-one suggests that a great deal of artistic ability is not involved along with some incredible craftsmanship, but the whole business of winemaking can now be strictly controlled, from the creating of the soil conditions for growing the grapes to the bottling of the finished product.

I do not care much for game or fish cooked in wine. That is a personal choice and I have no quarrel with those who do.

I enjoy wines to drink. I am not a connoisseur but I can tell a good quality wine from a supermarket plonk and I am confident that I can produce wines from various country sources that will leave some of the latter for dead!

Strictly speaking, of course, country wines are not wines. They are fermented juices of various kinds. Wine can only be made from grapes!

I believe, however, that game and fish dishes may be enhanced with a glass or two of wine (let us not be too fussy) from the hedgerow or wherever the raw materials are likely to be found. Without going overboard on the subject here (there are hundreds of excellent books around), I would like to touch briefly on a few of my own thoughts.

If we remember that sugar water turns to alcohol when yeast is added and fermentation takes place, it is not difficult to see that almost anything can be turned into an alcoholic drink. The flavour of the base product remains present and flavoured sugar water becomes flavoured alcohol. We need, however, a great deal more than that for an enjoyable wine-like drink.

When the Lord gave us grapes, he gave us all we needed to make wine. Even the yeast is present on the skin "bloom".

There is flavour, vinosity, acid of several kinds, sugar (in a special form) and tannin present in grapes. All of which combine to give us bouquet, flavour, taste and aftertaste. Those properties that are missing from country wines have to be added to make the end product palatable.

If, for instance, we make a wine from elderflower heads, we shall have bouquet, flavour of a kind, and an alcohol content. We need some additions to convert it into a wine-like substance.

In years past the vinosity was added in the form of raisins. The acids were added in the form of lemon or orange juice and zest and the tannin was often not considered at all. Yeast was, as often as not, baker's yeast left floating on a slice of toast, and the whole business was very much hit-and-miss.

Today we have grape concentrates of all kinds to improve the vinosity of country wines and to dispense with the need for raisins. We have citric, malic, tartaric and other acids in crystal form to add as we see fit. We have tannin tablets (or we may use strong cold tea!) to make up for any deficiency. And we have yeast cultures that are strong and virile enough to ensure complete fermentation. It is, therefore, possible, with the use of sterilized equipment (sodium metabisulphite, better known as camden tablets!) and air-locked casks or demijohns, to produce excellent country wines.

There are, as I have already indicated, many excellent books on the subject of home wine making. I do not wish to compete with those, even assuming I was capable of doing so. I simply wish here to encourage the reader to have a try at home wine production.

Knowing where to start is indeed a problem. There are so many raw materials to consider. My own two favourites happen to be elderflower, the so-called queen of wines as a white and a mixture of blackberry and elderberry as a red. Both are dependent upon a percentage of grape concentrate and an appropriate yeast. How much concentrate depends upon how much 'quality' is required in the end product.

If you are prepared to speculate on sufficient concentrate to make, say, five gallons of white wine and you flavour this with the juice from five pints of elder florets, you will have a superb wine for fish and white meat dishes.

All you do is pour several quarts of boiling water over the florets, let them steep overnight, and use the juice in the maker's recipe as outlined on the tin. Yeast, of course, as recommended. If you reduce the quantity of concentrate (down to as low as one fifth) you will have to add a teaspoon of citric acid, about $2\frac{1}{2}$ lb. of sugar, and a tablespoon of strong tea to each gallon of fermented juice. It is easy to experiment and adjust the finished wine but it should be remembered that it may take almost a year for the cheaper version to ferment out to dryness. Read the instructions on the can and 'do your own thing'. It's fun learning and books on the subject are cheap enough.

My own choice of a fruity red wine is made from equal quantities of blackberry, elderberry and red grape concentrate. I put down 15 gallons by the simple process of putting the juice from 15 lb. of blackberry, 15 lb. of elderberry and one five-gallon can of concentrate into a 15-gallon ferment. The juice is extracted from the berries by pouring over the correct amount of boiling water and straining after twenty-four hours or so. Sugar is then added and it is all made up to fifteen gallons (slightly more) by the concentrate and more water. When cooled to so-called blood heat, yeast is added, an airlock is fitted and the whole is fermented out to dryness. Acid adjustments may be made later; tannin content should be perfect since blackberries contain little or none and elderberries contain too much.

These are only basic suggestions but they may be applied to all kinds of wines from rose hip to rowan berry, and dandelion to damson or to blends of any or all.

Today's wine-making products are so totally professional that failure to produce an excellent product is almost out of the question. I have enjoyed many years of happy hunting and harvesting the good things of life and I am sure that anything I can do you can do better. But be warned. It is time-consuming and no respecter of a man's leisure.

LAST SEASONINGS AND
REASONINGS

THIS BOOK has to end somewhere and it is, perhaps, fitting to
end it here. It is incomplete, but it would still be incomplete a year
and ten more chapters from now. It can never be truly finished;
simply wound up at an appropriate spot. If I attempted to make it
utterly complete I would have to try and include 'exotic' game birds
like blackcock and capercaillie, of which I have no experience. I
would have to discuss moorhen and coot, which I have eaten and
enjoyed many times but which, in recent years, I have not shot.
These birds suffered heavy casualties during the 1963 freeze-up,
and although their numbers are now back to normal, the instinct to

preserve them has stayed with me. Many of the recipes suggested for rabbit, squirrel, and pigeon are, however, suitable.

Many birds of the shoreline, though edible, have been omitted for reasons best known to true wild fowlers.

The sea angler is, of course, a sportsman on a par with the freshwater angler; indeed many practise both sports regularly. If a complete chapter is missing, it is one concerning sea fish, but, with a few exceptions, the fish recipes in this book will apply to most sea fish. I am a comparative novice at sea, and my catches have been limited to whiting, cod, pollack, bass, bream, conger and dogfish. I have also caught mullet in the estuaries of several rivers and I have eaten all the sea fish I have caught except conger eel. I have friends who tell me that I have no soul and that they are delicious to eat, but as I have not cooked them myself nor sampled them to give an opinion, I cannot comment. I am convinced - no, I am sure - that the recipes for the various freshwater fish included in the foregoing chapters offer great scope for imagination and application to a vast number of sea fish. Turbot, halibut, and other less common sea fish may deserve better recipes than I have outlined, but they will not be ruined if cooked in the sauces I have described for other fish.

I ask the sea anglers' forgiveness for being so brief and offer as an excuse my lack of sea experience, a hatred of rough seas, and a landlubber's stomach. May I offer instead a hope for fair winds, easy tides, good marks and great catches. I envy you for your freshly caught sea fish and I know that there is no comparison between those and the trawler-caught fish obtained from retail outlets. May you long continue to catch, cook and eat your fish on the same day. 'And much good do you.'